The Dating Detox

Out of Your Type into Your Person.
Break toxic dating cycles.
Rewire your heart. Find real, healthy love.

Jed Lindsay.

Published by Eden Ray Publishing LTD

© Copyright 2025 - All rights reserved.

The content contained within this book may not be reproduced, duplicated or transmitted without direct written permission from the author or the publisher.

Under no circumstances will any blame or legal responsibility be held against the publisher, or author, for any damages, reparation, or monetary loss due to the information contained within this book, either directly or indirectly.

Legal Notice:

This book is copyright protected. It is only for personal use. You cannot amend, distribute, sell, use, quote or paraphrase any part, or the content within this book, without the consent of the author or publisher.

Disclaimer Notice:

Please note the information contained within this document is for educational and entertainment purposes only. All effort has been executed to present accurate, up to date, reliable, complete information. No warranties of any kind are declared or implied. Readers acknowledge that the author is not engaged in the rendering of legal, financial, medical or professional advice. The content within this book has been derived from various sources. Please consult a licensed professional before attempting any techniques outlined in this book.

By reading this document, the reader agrees that under no circumstances is the author responsible for any losses, direct or indirect, that are incurred as a result of the use of the information contained within this document, including, but not limited to, errors, omissions, or inaccuracies.

A Note to You (Yes, You!)

Dear Reader,

First off, thank you for picking up this book. No, really – thank you. In a world where you could be doom-scrolling through Instagram, watching strangers dancing on TikTok, or shopping for things you don't need during a late-night impulse spending spree, you chose to invest in yourself instead. That's quite a significant development.

I'm not going to pretend this was an easy book to write. There were days when my laptop and I had serious relationship issues. Days when I wondered if anyone would even care about what I had to say about dating. Days when I ordered takeout for the third time that week and called it "writing fuel" while staring at a blank document— I regret nothing.

But then I'd remember all the 3 AM conversations with friends about their latest dating disasters. The tearful phone calls after another ghosting incident. The collective sigh that follows when someone asks, "So, how's the dating life?" at family gatherings. And I kept writing.

Dating is strange. It's this odd social ritual where we dress a bit better than usual, spend too much on drinks, and try to figure out if this person might be someone we eventually want to share a Netflix account with. Upon reflection, the entire process seems quite absurd.

And yet, here we are – still hoping, trying, believing that somewhere in this messy, complicated world, there is someone who will love us exactly as we are. Someone who will make us laugh until our abs hurt. Someone who will hold our hand through the hard stuff and dance with us through the good.

That's why I wrote this book. Not because I have all the answers (spoiler: I don't), but because I believe we can approach dating with more intention, more self-awareness, and, yes, more humour.

As you read, I hope you'll laugh a little, cringe in recognition at times, perhaps shed a tear or two, and ultimately feel less alone on this wild journey called dating.

You've got this. We've got this—one awkward date at a time.

With love and solidarity,

Jed Lindsay.

P.S. If this book is currently serving as a coaster for your coffee cup while you swipe through dating apps... well, at least it's multitasking, just like you.

Table Of Contents

INTRODUCTION 1
   THE MODERN DATING CRISIS 1
   WHY TRADITIONAL DATING ADVICE FAILS 4
   SO, WHAT WORKS? 7
   THE DATING DETOX PHILOSOPHY 8

HOW TO USE THIS BOOK 11
   STEP 1: COMMIT TO THE FULL PROCESS 12
   STEP 2: CREATE A DATING DETOX JOURNAL 12
   STEP 3: READ AT YOUR OWN PACE (BUT DO THE WORK) 13
   STEP 4: FIND AN ACCOUNTABILITY PARTNER (OPTIONAL BUT RECOMMENDED)... 13
   STEP 5: BE GENTLE WITH YOURSELF 14
      Final Thoughts Before We Begin... *15*
   CASE STUDIES: THREE COMMON PATTERN TYPES 15
      Why These Patterns Matter... *19*

CHAPTER 1: RELATIONSHIP ARCHAEOLOGY 21
   DIGGING INTO YOUR SHARED STORY: RELATIONSHIP ARCHAEOLOGY 22
   UNDERSTANDING YOUR ATTACHMENT STYLE 23
   THE IMPACT OF EARLY RELATIONSHIPS ON PARTNER SELECTION 25
   IDENTIFY YOUR UNIQUE RELATIONSHIP PATTERNS 28
   CASE STUDIES: THESE COMMON TYPES 30
      The Anxious Pursuer *30*
      The Avoidant Distancer... *31*
      The Secure Base *32*
      The Anxious-Avoidant Trap... *32*
      The People-Pleaser *33*
      The Relationship Saboteur.. *33*
      The Relationship Renovator.. *34*
   SELF-ASSESSMENT: MAPPING YOUR RELATIONSHIP HISTORY 35
      Step 1: Create Your Relationship Map *35*
      Step 2: Identify Your Patterns *36*
      Step 3: Connect the Dots to Your Early Attachments *37*
      Step 4: Identify Your Attachment Triggers *38*
      Step 5: Recognize Your Protest Behaviours *38*
      Step 6: Write Your Relationship Story (Then Rewrite It) *39*

    Step 7: Compassionate Awareness.. 39
RESEARCH SPOTLIGHT: THE WORK OF DR. JOHN GOTTMAN ON RELATIONSHIP
PATTERNS... 40
    The Love Lab Revolution 40
    The Four Horsemen of the Relationship Apocalypse 41
    The Magic Relationship Ratio: 5:1 42
    Bids for Connection... 42
    Relationship Masters vs. Disasters 43
    Practical Applications 44

CHAPTER 2: THE ATTRACTION TRAP 47

    WHY WE'RE DRAWN TO THE WRONG PEOPLE... 47
    WHY WE'RE ALL MEMBERS OF THE "WHAT'S WRONG WITH ME?" CLUB......... 47
    BETTER QUESTIONS THAT WON'T MAKE YOUR THERAPIST SIGH 48
    THE HEALTHY RELATIONSHIP WITH YOURSELF CHECKLIST 49
    THE NEUROCHEMISTRY OF UNHEALTHY ATTRACTION 51
        Your Brain's Drug Dealer: Meet the Reward System 52
        Dopamine: The Chemical Culprit Behind "I Can't Stop Thinking
        About Them" 52
        Oxytocin: The Attachment Accelerator.. 53
        Cortisol: The Stress Hormone That Keeps You Coming Back 54
        Adrenaline: Mistaking Fear for Love.. 54
        Breaking the Chemical Addiction to Unhealthy Relationships....... 55
    RED FLAGS VS. GREEN FLAGS: A COMPLETE GUIDE 56
        What Are Relationship Flags? 56
        Communication Flags 57
        Emotional Intelligence Flags... 59
        Respect Flags.. 61
        Trust Flags 62
        Independence/Interdependence Flags 64
        Conflict Resolution Flags 65
        Personal Growth Flags... 67
        Practical Living Flags 68
        Inner Circle Flags 70
        Relationship Experience Flags 71
        Value Alignment Flags... 73
        Flag Interpretation Guidelines... 74
        Final Thoughts: Your Personal Flag System 75
    BREAKING THE CHEMISTRY ADDICTION 76
        Step 1: Decode Your Chemistry Pattern... 77
        Step 2: Recognize Chemistry vs. Compatibility 77

Step 3: Implement the Attraction Intervention 78
Step 4: Install New Attraction Software 80
Step 5: Manage the Withdrawal Period 81
Step 6: Celebrate New Patterns 82
RESEARCH SPOTLIGHT: STUDIES ON RELATIONSHIP SATISFACTION VS. INITIAL ATTRACTION 84
PRACTICAL TOOL: THE ATTRACTION RESET PROTOCOL 86
    PHASE 1: PATTERN MAPPING (Duration: 1-2 Weeks) 86
    PHASE 2: REWIRING TRIGGERS (Duration: 2-4 Weeks) 87
    PHASE 3: RECALIBRATING STANDARDS (Duration: 2-4 Weeks) 89
    PHASE 4: SUSTAINABLE INTEGRATION (Duration: Ongoing) 91

CHAPTER 3: YOUR DATING BLIND SPOTS 95

WHAT YOU CAN'T SEE MIGHT BE HURTING YOU 95
    The Science of Selective Vision 95
COMMON DATING BLIND SPOTS (AND YES, YOU PROBABLY HAVE AT LEAST ONE) 96
HOW TO ILLUMINATE YOUR BLIND SPOTS 103
THE ULTIMATE BLIND SPOT: THINKING IT'S JUST ABOUT FINDING THE "RIGHT PERSON" 106
COMMON COGNITIVE BIASES IN PARTNER SELECTION 107
THE ROLE OF SELF-SABOTAGE IN DATING 108
    What Is Self-Sabotage, exactly? 109
IDENTIFYING YOUR PERSONAL DATING MYTHS 110
    Common Dating Myths That Might Be Limiting You 110
EXERCISE: THE RELATIONSHIP REALITY CHECK 111
EXPERT INTERVIEWS: THERAPISTS ON BREAKING CYCLES 113
RESEARCH SPOTLIGHT: COGNITIVE BEHAVIOURAL APPROACHES TO DATING 115
    The Cognitive Foundation of Dating Behaviours 115

CHAPTER 4: THE DETOX PERIOD 117

WHEN BREAKING BAD PATTERNS FEELS WORSE BEFORE IT GETS BETTER 117
THE SCIENCE OF HABIT BREAKING 120
    Why Your Brain Is Addicted to Your Dating Patterns 121
    Creating Your Dating Sabbatical 121
PLANNING YOUR PERSONALIZED DETOX PROTOCOL 122
    Step 1: Define Your Specific Parameters 122
    Step 2: Set Your Duration and Intention 123
    Step 3: Prepare Your Environment 124
    Step 4: Design Your Replacement Activities 126
    Step 5: Establish Your Support System 128

  Step 6: Track Your Progress and Insights 129
  Step 7: Plan Your Reintegration Strategy 130
 THE REALITY CHECK: EXPECT CHALLENGES 131
 CREATING NEW NEURAL PATHWAYS 132
  The Neuroscience of Building New Pathways 133
  The Building Blocks of New Neural Pathways 134
 JOURNALING PROMPTS FOR THE DETOX PHASE 135
  Week One: Pattern Recognition Prompts 136
  Week Two: Origins & Influences Prompts 137
  Week Three: Needs & Desires Prompts 138
  Week Four: Attachment & Triggers Prompts 138
  Week Five: Values & Boundaries Prompts 139
  Week Six: Integration & Moving Forward Prompts 140
 RESEARCH SPOTLIGHT: STUDIES ON HABIT FORMATION AND CHANGE 141
 CASE STUDIES: SUCCESS STORIES FROM THE DETOX PERIOD 143

CHAPTER 5: DATING YOURSELF FIRST 149

 SELF-RELATIONSHIP AS THE FOUNDATION 149
 DEVELOPING SELF-COMPASSION AND WORTH 150
  The Science of Self-Compassion 150
 BREAKING THE WORTHINESS-ACHIEVEMENT LINK 152
 PRACTICAL SELF-COMPASSION EXERCISES 152
 DESIGNING A LIFE THAT ATTRACTS THE RIGHT PARTNER 153
  The Magnetic Effect of an Authentic Life 154
  The Fulfilment Gap 155
  The Full Life Inventory 155
  The Partner Prototype vs. Relationship Vision Distinction 156
 EXERCISE: THE IDEAL RELATIONSHIP WITH YOURSELF 157
 RESEARCH SPOTLIGHT: SELF-DETERMINATION THEORY AND RELATIONSHIP SUCCESS
 160
 PRACTICAL TOOL: THE SELF-DATING CALENDAR 167
  Weekly Connection Dates: Developing the Relationship 169
  Monthly Deep Dive Dates: Transformative Experiences 171

CHAPTER 6: HEALING YOUR RELATIONSHIP WITH LOVE 175

 PROCESSING PAST RELATIONSHIP TRAUMA 175
 HOW PAST WOUNDS BECOME PRESENT PATTERNS 176
 THE PHYSICAL REALITY OF EMOTIONAL WOUNDS 177
 FORGIVING OTHERS (AND YOURSELF) 178
  What Forgiveness Is (and isn't) 179
 THE FORGIVENESS PROCESS: PRACTICAL STEPS 181

THE FREEDOM OF RELEASE 184
REBUILDING TRUST IN THE PROCESS OF LOVE 185
RECLAIMING YOUR CAPACITY FOR CONNECTION 186
EXERCISE: THE LETTER YOU'LL NEVER SEND 188
EXPERT INTERVIEWS: TRAUMA SPECIALISTS ON RELATIONSHIP HEALING 192
RESEARCH SPOTLIGHT: POST-TRAUMATIC RELATIONSHIP GROWTH 194

CHAPTER 7: BUILDING YOUR SUPPORT SYSTEM 199

THE ROLE OF COMMUNITY IN HEALTHY DATING 199
THE PRESSURE COOKER OF ROMANTIC ISOLATION 200
THE RESEARCH ON RELATIONSHIP SUSTAINABILITY 201
THE FOUNDATION TRIANGLE: SELF, COMMUNITY, PARTNER 202
CREATING ACCOUNTABILITY 203
    Why You Need Dating Accountability Partners 203
    Selecting the Right Accountability Partners 204
    Structured Accountability That Works 205
SELECTING DATING MENTORS AND ADVISORS 207
EXERCISE: MAPPING YOUR SUPPORT NETWORK 211
RESEARCH SPOTLIGHT: SOCIAL NETWORK EFFECTS ON RELATIONSHIP QUALITY . 215
CASE STUDIES: HOW COMMUNITY CHANGES DATING OUTCOMES 220
PRACTICAL TOOL: THE SUPPORT SYSTEM DESIGN WORKSHOP 227

CHAPTER 8: STRATEGIC DATING 235

FROM DATING DISASTER TO DATING MASTERMIND 235
INTENTIONAL VS. PASSIVE PARTNER FINDING: CHOOSE YOUR ADVENTURE 235
THE MINDSET SHIFT: FROM HOPEFUL ROMANTIC TO LOVE STRATEGIST 236
THE FOUR COMPONENTS OF STRATEGIC DATING (NO MBA REQUIRED) 238
ONLINE AND OFFLINE DATING STRATEGIES: A FOOT IN BOTH WORLDS 239
THE QUALITY OVER QUANTITY APPROACH (STOP DATING LIKE YOU'RE SAMPLING FREE CHEESE AT COSTCO) 247
YOUR PERSONAL DATING PLAN: FROM CHAOS TO STRATEGY 254
THE RESEARCH SHOWS: DATING SMARTER WORKS 255
THE DATING EFFICIENCY MATRIX: WORK SMARTER, NOT HARDER 256
BALANCING EFFICIENCY AND SERENDIPITY: LEAVE ROOM FOR MAGIC 257

CHAPTER 9: AUTHENTIC CONNECTION SKILLS - THE ART OF NOT BEING AWKWARD 259

THE SCIENCE OF DEEP BONDING (WITHOUT THE LAB COAT) 259
THE CONNECTION PARADOX (OR WHY THIS STUFF IS SO CONFUSING) 260
THE THREE LEVELS OF CONNECTION (BECAUSE EVERYTHING NEEDS LEVELS) 260
WHY CONNECTION SKILLS MATTER MORE THAN EVER (BLAME THE APPS) 262

VULNERABILITY WITHOUT OVERSHARING (OR: HOW NOT TO TRAUMA DUMP ON DATE ONE) 263
    The Vulnerability Spectrum 264
    The Four Components of Healthy Vulnerability 265
    Practical Vulnerability Techniques 268
MEANINGFUL CONVERSATION TECHNIQUES (BEYOND "WHAT DO YOU DO?"). 270
EXERCISE: THE ESCALATING INTIMACY PRACTICE (NO, NOT THAT KIND OF INTIMACY) 277
EXPERT INTERVIEWS: COMMUNICATION SPECIALISTS (BECAUSE WHY NOT GET SOME PRO TIPS?) 281
THE CONTINUOUS CONNECTION PRACTICE (BECAUSE THIS ISN'T A ONE-AND-DONE DEAL) 285
CUSTOMISING YOUR CONNECTION APPROACH (BECAUSE YOU'RE UNIQUELY YOU) 291
WHEN CONNECTION DOESN'T DEVELOP (SOMETIMES IT'S JUST NOT THERE) ... 293

CHAPTER 10: EVALUATING COMPATIBILITY 295

BEYOND CHEMISTRY: THE FOUR PILLARS OF COMPATIBILITY.......................... 295
PILLAR 1: VALUES COMPATIBILITY 296
PILLAR 2: EMOTIONAL COMPATIBILITY 298
PILLAR 3: PRACTICAL/LIFESTYLE COMPATIBILITY 299
PILLAR 4: PHYSICAL/SEXUAL COMPATIBILITY 301
THE COMPATIBILITY ASSESSMENT MATRIX 302
RED FLAGS VS. GROWTH OPPORTUNITIES 304
WHEN TO STAY AND WHEN TO MOVE ON 311
EXERCISE: THE THREE-DATE ASSESSMENT METHOD 318
RESEARCH SPOTLIGHT: WHAT ACTUALLY PREDICTS RELATIONSHIP SUCCESS? ... 323
PRACTICAL TOOL: YOUR COMPATIBILITY EVALUATION TOOLKIT 325

CHAPTER 11: FROM DATING TO RELATIONSHIP 327

NAVIGATING THE AWKWARD MIDDLE SPACE (WITHOUT LOSING YOUR MIND). 327
WELCOME TO RELATIONSHIP LIMBO 328
THE TRANSITION TRAPS THAT'LL GET YOU EVERY TIME 329
THE INTENTIONAL TRANSITION: A BETTER WAY FORWARD 330
BUILDING A FOUNDATION THAT WON'T COLLAPSE UNDER PRESSURE 332
CREATING A RELATIONSHIP AGREEMENT (WITHOUT FEELING LIKE YOU'RE SIGNING UP FOR A CELL PHONE PLAN) 335
MAINTAINING YOUR AUTHENTIC SELF (BECAUSE YOU'VE WORKED TOO HARD TO LOSE YOURSELF NOW) 336
REAL COUPLES, REAL TRANSITIONS... 338
THE SCIENCE BEHIND SUCCESSFUL TRANSITIONS 339

    Your Transition Toolkit: A Practical Exercise 340

CONCLUSION **343**

    The Path You've Travelled 343
    From Reactive to Intentional... 344
    The Ongoing Practice 345
    Beyond the Book... 345
    Your Continuing Journey.. 346

APPENDICES **351**

Introduction

The Modern Dating Crisis

Let's be honest: dating in the twenty-first century feels like trying to solve a Rubik's Cube while blindfolded, riding a unicycle, and being chased by geese.

If you've recently found yourself at 3 AM, illuminated only by the harsh glow of your phone screen, thumb hovering indecisively over another dating profile while wondering, "How did dating get this complicated?" — congratulations! You've joined the rest of us in what I affectionately call "The Great Dating Dumpster Fire of the Modern Age."

I didn't set out to write this book. In fact, after my third consecutive relationship that ended with me ugly-crying into a pint of ice cream while my best friend patiently reminded me that "he wasn't even my type," I was ready to adopt seventeen cats and call it a life. Dating felt like a game where the rules kept changing, nobody told me about the updates, and occasionally, someone would flip the board over entirely.

Maybe you know the feeling.

Perhaps you've found yourself explaining to well-meaning relatives at Thanksgiving dinner that, no, you haven't met "The One" yet. Yes, you are trying, and no, lowering your standards to include "anyone with a pulse" isn't helpful advice. (Thanks, Uncle Frank.)

Or perhaps you've had the distinct pleasure of receiving that unique "we need to talk" text while shopping for his or her birthday present. Or realised you've gone on so many first dates that you've accidentally told the same "funny story about your college roommate" to the same person on two separate occasions. (True story. Not mine. A friend. Okay, fine, it was me.)

Yet here's the paradox: we're more connected than ever, but meaningful connection feels increasingly rare. We have apps that can deliver food, movies, and potential soulmates to our doorstep with a few taps, yet finding someone who makes your heart skip a beat feels harder than explaining TikTok to your grandparents.

Dating apps promise to revolutionise romance. Finally, a way to meet people beyond your immediate social circle! The possibilities seemed endless. Instead, many of us find ourselves trapped in an infinite cycle of swiping, messaging, meeting, being disappointed, and repeating. Dating has become both more accessible and, at the same time, infinitely more complicated.

"But people have always complained about dating," you might say. True. I'm sure even cave people had awkward first dates. ("I think your club is very impressive. You want to share mammoth meat?")

The difference is that today's dating landscape is shaped by unprecedented forces: technology that allows us to meet more people while knowing them less, social media that turns relationships into public performances, and a culture that struggles to decide whether it wants casual hookups or fairytale romances.

And don't get me started on the mixed messages. Society tells us to be authentic but not too genuine. Be confident but not arrogant. Be emotionally open, but avoid rapid attachment. Maintain composure while remaining open and approachable. It's like trying to follow a recipe where half the instructions are written in hieroglyphics, and the other half contradict each other.

I've spent the last five years interviewing hundreds of fellow dating warriors, relationship experts, psychologists, and even a few happily married couples (whom I only slightly resent for figuring it out). I've analysed data from dating apps, examined cultural shifts in relationship formation, and, yes, conducted extensive "field research" that wasn't just me going on terrible dates and calling it work.

What I discovered surprised me. Behind all the frustration, miscommunication, and dating horror stories lies something unexpected: hope. Because despite everything, we keep trying. We download yet another app. We agree to be set up by that friend who swears, "This one is different." We put on nice clothes and show up again and again.

Why? Because connection matters. Finding someone who gets your weird jokes, holds your hand during scary movies, knows precisely how you like your coffee, and chooses you – day after day – is still worth pursuing, even if the journey is messy.

This book isn't about game-playing or manipulation tactics. It's not about settling or lowering your standards. And it's not about making yourself more appealing by becoming less yourself. Instead, it's about navigating modern dating with your sanity, mostly, intact. It's about understanding the new rules while refusing to play games that don't serve you. It's about finding genuine connections in an age of superficial swipes. And most importantly, it's about approaching the whole chaotic mess with a sense of humour because sometimes laughing is better than curling up with a comfortable movie marathon. (Though if binge-watching romantic comedies is your coping mechanism, I fully support it. Just save a spot on the couch for me.)

This book is for you, whether you're swiping right, sliding into DMs, or still trying to meet people the old-fashioned way—making awkward eye contact at the grocery store. Let's figure out this dating thing together – no perfect answers guaranteed, but plenty of solidarity, insight, and hopefully a few laughs along the way.

Welcome to "Swipe Right on Sanity: Navigating Love in the Digital Age." Let's begin.

Why Traditional Dating Advice Fails

Let's talk about traditional dating advice, shall we? You know, those well-meaning nuggets of wisdom that your mom, magazines, and that one friend who's been in a relationship since high school keep feeding you.

"Just be yourself!" "Put yourself out there more!" "The right person will come along when you stop looking!" "Have you tried Pilates? I met my husband at a Pilates class.

I don't know about you, but my favourite is "Plenty of Fish in the Sea." It's as if the problem is that I haven't noticed the vast ocean of dating possibilities surrounding me. "Oh, fish? In the sea? Why didn't anyone mention this before? I've been looking in the desert this whole time!"

The truth is most dating advice fails spectacularly for a few key reasons:

It's Comically Generic

Traditional dating advice treats love like a fast-food menu – as if everyone wants the same burger and the preparation method never changes. "Dress nicely, maintain eye contact, and ask questions about them." Thanks, I hadn't considered the revolutionary strategy of looking at my date.

What this advice misses is that you're not generic. Your relationship patterns, attachment style, values, and needs are as unique as your fingerprint. Telling everyone to "just be confident" is like telling everyone the secret to basketball success is "just be tall." It is helpful for some but physiologically impossible for others.

It Treats Symptoms, Not Causes

Mainstream dating advice is phenomenal at addressing the surface-level symptoms of dating problems rather than their root causes.

Having trouble getting second dates? Here's how to be more interesting! Keep attracting unavailable partners? Here's how to seem more desirable! Is relationship anxiety ruining your connections? Here are seven things you should say to keep them interested!

This is like treating a broken leg with a Band-Aid. Sure, the Band-Aid is nice, but you still can't walk.

It Ignores Modern Reality

The dating landscape has undergone seismic shifts, yet much of the conventional wisdom remains stubbornly anchored in a pre-digital era. "Just go where single people hang out" might have been sound advice when community dances were the hotspot for meeting potential partners. Now? The most populous gathering place for singles is the glowing rectangle in your hand.

Traditional advice rarely accounts for how dating apps have fundamentally altered the process of relationship formation, the paradox of choice that comes with seemingly infinite options, or how social media has transformed courtship into a multi-platform performance. It's like applying medieval battle tactics to modern workplace conflicts—interesting historically but not particularly applicable.

It Assumes a Predetermined Journey

Perhaps the most frustrating assumption baked into traditional dating advice is that relationships follow a predictable, linear progression: meet, date, commit, marry, reproduce. This cookie-cutter template ignores the beautiful diversity of human connection.

Many of us are crafting relationships that don't fit neatly into conventional boxes. Some are opting for ethical non-monogamy, while others prioritise emotional connection without traditional commitment structures, and many are redefining what partnership means altogether. Traditional advice often treats these variations as either temporary phases or failures rather than valid relationship models.

It's Steeped in Outdated Gender Roles

"Men should always pay on the first date." "Don't text him first." "Make him chase you." "Don't seem too eager." "Don't call him." What about our same-sex partners, who are both men? Who should pay for the date then?

This highlights a perfect example of how traditional dating advice often fails to consider relationships outside the heteronormative framework. When both partners are men, the old rules that assign roles based on gender simply don't apply. This forces couples to create their guidelines based on mutual respect and communication rather than outdated gender expectations—something that would benefit all relationships regardless of sexual orientation.

If I had a dollar for every piece of gendered dating advice I've encountered, I could retire to a private island where I'd never have to hear the phrase "playing hard to get" again. Much traditional wisdom remains mired in rigid gender expectations that feel increasingly disconnected from how many of us experience gender and relationships.

These outdated rules create unnecessary games and power dynamics rather than fostering authentic connections. They assume heteronormativity and traditional gender expression in ways that exclude many people's lived experiences.

So, What Works?

If you're feeling frustrated by now, that's understandable. I've just dismantled most of the dating advice you've likely received throughout your life without offering alternatives. Don't worry—the rest of this book will fill that void. But first, we need to establish some foundational principles that genuinely support healthy relationship formation:

1. **Self-knowledge trumps dating techniques**. Understanding your attachment patterns, emotional triggers, and relationship needs will take you further than mastering any flirting technique.

2. **Authenticity creates sustainability**. Relationships built on performance inevitably collapse when the show becomes too exhausting to maintain.

3. **Connection is contextual**. What works for one person or relationship might be disastrous for another. Some principles promote healthy relationships, but there is no universal formula.

4. **Dating is not just about finding someone—it's about becoming someone** worth being with. The journey shapes you as much as it leads you to others.

Throughout this book, we'll explore these principles in depth, offering practical strategies that acknowledge the complexities of modern connection while honouring the timeless human need for love and belonging.

So, let's leave behind outdated scripts and oversimplified solutions. It's time to develop a more nuanced, personalised approach to finding connection in this strange new dating landscape—one that reflects the world we're living in, not the one our parents navigated decades ago.

The Dating Detox Philosophy

So, what exactly is a Dating Detox, and why am I suggesting you need one? Am I about to recommend a 10-day juice cleanse for your love life? Will you need to carry crystals and chant affirmations at the moon? (Spoiler: no, though if that's your thing, you do you.)

The Dating Detox Philosophy is simple, though the process can be challenging. It's built on a simple premise:

Your dating life mirrors your self-relationship.

I know, I know. That sounds like something you'd find cross-stitched on a pillow in the self-help section of a discount store. However, stay with me because beneath this seemingly trite statement lies a powerful truth that science is increasingly supporting.

The Dating Detox approach is built on four core principles:

1. Patterns, Not People

Most of us blame our dating struggles on the people we've dated:

Men in this city are often commitment-phobic. "All the good women are taken." "Dating apps are full of narcissists."

While there may be grains of truth in these statements (looking at you, a guy who showed up to our date with a spreadsheet ranking all his active Tinder matches), they miss something crucial: **the common denominator in all your relationships is you.**

This isn't about blame. It's about power. When you recognise that you're continuously attracted to or attracting certain types of people or situations, you gain the power to change the pattern rather than just avoiding the next person who might fit it.

The core premise—that your dating life reflects your relationship with yourself—is indeed powerful. Instead of attributing dating struggles to other people or circumstances ("commitment-phobic men," "all good women are taken," etc.), the philosophy encourages looking inward at the patterns you participate in.

I particularly like the framing that recognising your role in relationship patterns isn't about blame but about power. When you acknowledge that you're the common denominator in your relationships, you can change those patterns rather than avoid the next person who might fit them.

How to Use This Book

Congratulations! You've now acquired a dating book that doesn't promise to turn you into a "man magnet" or teach you " 3 texts that will make her obsessed with you." I consider this progress already.

But you might be wondering: how exactly should I use this book? Read it cover-to-cover in one sitting. Treat it like a workbook? Use it as a coaster for drinks while you swipe through dating apps. (Please don't do the last one. I worked hard on this, and electronics and liquids don't mix.)

Here's my recommendation for getting the most out of your Dating Detox journey:

This Isn't a Normal Book (Sorry Not Sorry)

First, let's establish what this book is not: it's not a passive reading experience. If you're looking for something to breeze through on the beach this summer, may I suggest a nice thriller instead?

Dating Detox is part story, part science, and a whole lot of roll up your sleeves and do the work. The reading itself won't change your dating life any more than reading about push-ups will give you stronger arms. It's in the doing that transformation happens.

With that said, here's how to approach it:

Step 1: Commit to the Full Process

The Dating Detox method functions as a comprehensive system, not a buffet, where you pick and choose the parts that sound appealing. (If that were the case, we'd all skip to the "Finding Your Person" section and call it a day, right?)

Before you begin, commit to:

- Reading all three sections in order

- Completing the exercises (even the uncomfortable ones)

- Taking the recommended 30–90-day dating sabbatical

- Being ruthlessly honest with yourself throughout the process

Step 2: Create a Dating Detox Journal

You'll need a dedicated notebook or digital document to complete the exercises in this book. I call this your "Dating Detox Journal," and it's where the real magic happens. Your journal is a judgment-free zone where you can be completely honest with yourself.

Why write things down instead of just thinking about them? Because there's something powerful about externalising your thoughts. Writing creates clarity, reveals patterns you might miss otherwise, and holds you accountable to yourself. Plus, it's fascinating to look back later and see how much your perspective has evolved.

Pro tip: Choose a journal format that feels good to you. If you're a digital person, create a password-protected document. If you're old-school like me, get a physical notebook that brings you joy when you see it. (Yes, I Marie Kondo'd my journaling process. No regrets.)

Step 3: Read at Your Own Pace (But Do the Work)

Some chapters will resonate deeply, and you'll want to linger there. Others might trigger resistance or feel less relevant to your situation. That's all normal. Take your time with the material that resonates with you, but don't skip the sections that make you uncomfortable—that's often where the biggest breakthroughs lie.

I recommend reading each chapter first without doing the exercises to absorb the concepts. Then, go back and work through the exercises when you're ready to engage more deeply.

Give yourself at least a week with each major section. Speed doesn't equal quality. Relationship patterns formed over decades aren't rewritten overnight.

Step 4: Find an Accountability Partner (Optional but Recommended)

Change is easier with support. Consider finding a friend who's also interested in improving their relationship with dating to join you on this journey. You can discuss insights, share experiences, and encourage each other through the challenging parts.

If you don't have someone in mind, there's an online community of fellow Dating Detoxers where you can connect with others on the same path. Sometimes, it's easier to be vulnerable with strangers who understand precisely what you're going through.

Step 5: Be Gentle with Yourself

This process will bring up stuff. Uncomfortable realisations. Old wounds. Patterns you didn't know you had. When it does, remember that awareness is the first step toward change, and discomfort is often a sign of growth.

Practice self-compassion throughout this journey. You're not doing this because you're broken or defective. You're doing it because you're courageous enough to want more for yourself and your relationships.

A Note on Privacy

Some exercises will ask you to reflect on past relationships and patterns that might involve other people. A few guidelines:

1. This work is for you, not for confronting exes or people you've dated

2. Keep your journal private—these reflections aren't meant to be shared on social media

3. Focus on patterns and your responses rather than cataloguing others' faults

Final Thoughts Before We Begin

Dating Detox isn't about becoming a different person to attract love. It's about becoming more authentically yourself and creating space for meaningful connection. The goal isn't to make yourself more marketable in the dating economy—it's to break free from that mindset entirely.

Ready? Let's turn the page on your old dating story and start writing a new one.

Case Studies: Three Common Pattern Types

Let me introduce you to three people who don't exist but whom you'll probably recognise immediately. Perhaps in yourself, perhaps in a friend, or in that person you've been dating for the past three months who just left you on read for the fifth time this week. (Spoiler alert: They're not "just busy with work.")

These case studies represent three of the most common relationship patterns I've observed in my research. While everyone's story is unique, these archetypes appear so frequently that they're worth highlighting. As you read, notice which elements feel familiar. The point isn't to box yourself into a category but to start recognising patterns that might influence your dating life.

Pattern #1: The Anxious Pursuer (aka "Please Love Me Back")

Meet Morgan

Morgan is innovative, successful, and perpetually drawn to emotionally unavailable people. Their dating history reads like a catalogue of almost-relationships:

- Alex, who was "not ready for anything serious" but happy to text Morgan daily for eight months

- Jordan, who was technically still married but "emotionally separated"

- Taylor, who kept Morgan a secret from friends and family for reasons that were "complicated"

- Riley, who was "really into" Morgan but somehow never free on weekends

The pattern is consistent: Morgan is attracted to people who provide inconsistent attention. When they receive affection, they're elated. When it's withdrawn (regularly), they become anxious and enter pursuit mode—sending extra texts, planning elaborate dates, or simply ruminating obsessively about what they did wrong.

Friends tell Morgan to "have more self-respect" and "stop chasing people who don't value you." Morgan agrees intellectually but can't seem to generate the same chemistry with available, consistent partners. Those connections feel "boring" or "too easy," while the rollercoaster relationships feels "deep" and "real."

Pattern #2: The Avoidant Distancer (aka "I Need My Space")

Meet Jamie

Jamie is self-sufficient, independent, and allergic to clinginess. From the outside, Jamie appears to "have it all together" — a successful career, a stylish apartment, and a busy social life. Dating is something Jamie does casually when it fits into an already-packed schedule.

Jamie's relationship history is characterised by:

- Reese, who was "smothering" after wanting to spend three consecutive evenings together

- Devon, who became "too intense" after bringing up exclusivity two months in

- Casey, whose "neediness" became apparent after expecting good morning texts

- Skyler who was "basically perfect", but somehow Jamie felt "trapped" and had to end it

The pattern is subtle but persistent: Jamie craves connection but becomes uncomfortable when relationships deepen. The early stages are exciting, but as emotional intimacy increases, so does Jamie's anxiety. Minor irritations become magnified. The need for "space" grows urgent. Eventually, Jamie creates distance by picking fights, working longer hours, or ending the relationship directly.

When asked about ideal partnerships, Jamie uses words like "independent," "low maintenance," and "respectful of boundaries." Jamie is puzzled by friends who seem happily interdependent, suspecting they must be suppressing their actual needs or settling.

What others see as normal relationship progression, Jamie experiences as encroachment. The result is a series of connections that end just as they begin to develop depth, leaving Jamie simultaneously relieved and lonely.

Pattern #3: The Safety Seeker (aka "The Perfect Person Checklist")

Meet Charlie

Charlie is thoughtful, analytical, and determined not to waste time on the wrong person. Armed with hard-earned wisdom from past disappointments and an extensive mental checklist, Charlie approaches dating with the precision of a scientist.

Charlie's dating history includes:

- Rejecting Quinn after three great dates upon discovering their different views on having children

- Ending things with Addison after spotting a "red flag" in how they talked about their ex

- Not pursuing Morgan because their career wasn't stable enough

- Finding Avery nearly perfect but having "no spark" — despite compatibility on paper

Charlie's pattern revolves around protection from potential pain. Each past relationship has added new items to the checklist, making the criteria for a suitable partner increasingly specific. Dating has become less about connection and more about assessment.

Dates feel like interviews where Charlie is simultaneously the candidate and the hiring manager. The mental checklist runs constantly: Are they financially stable? Do they have a good relationship with their family? Are they emotionally intelligent? Are they adventurous but also reliable? Do they want the same things in the same timeline?

Charlie's friends describe them as "picky," but Charlie sees it as "having standards." The problem is that while this approach effectively screens out unsuitable matches, it also filters out potentially excellent connections that might not check every predefined box.

Charlie wants deep love but has built a fortress of requirements that few can penetrate. The result is safety from heartbreak but also protection from the vulnerability that meaningful connections require.

Why These Patterns Matter

These archetypes—the Anxious Pursuer, the Avoidant Distancer, and the Safety Seeker—represent common strategies we develop to protect ourselves in relationships. None of them are wrong or broken; they're adaptive responses to our experiences.

However, when these patterns operate unconsciously, they can sabotage our genuine desire for connection. The Anxious Pursuer exhausts themselves, chasing unavailable people. The Avoidant Distancer remains isolated despite craving closeness. The Safety Seeker remains safe but misses opportunities for growth and love.

As you read these descriptions, you might recognise elements of yourself in multiple patterns. That's normal. Most of us don't fit perfectly into one category, and our patterns can shift depending on who we're dating and what else is happening in our lives.

The question isn't "Which one am I?" but "Which behaviours do I notice in myself, and how might they affect my relationships?"

In the next section, we'll explore how to identify your patterns more specifically, understand their origins, and begin creating new, more fulfilling relationship dynamics.

However, first, consider this reflection question: Which case study resonated with you the most strongly, and why? Take a moment to write down your thoughts in your Dating Detox Journal.

CHAPTER 1:

Relationship Archaeology

Relationship archaeology is the practice of examining and exploring past interactions, patterns, and events in a relationship to better understand its dynamics, challenges, and foundations. Like traditional archaeologists, who uncover and study artefacts to learn about past civilisations, relationship archaeology involves digging through the "layers" of a relationship's history.

This approach can involve:

1. Identifying recurring patterns of communication or conflict

2. Exploring the origins of specific relationship dynamics or issues

3. Uncovering forgotten positive experiences or connections

4. Examining how past experiences have shaped current perceptions and reactions

5. Understanding the "relational artefacts" (significant moments, rituals, or shared experiences) that have built the relationship's foundation

Relationship archaeology can be practised in various contexts:

- In therapy or counselling settings, where professionals guide couples through examining their relationship history

- As a self-reflection tool for individuals wanting to understand their relationship patterns

- Between partners as a collaborative exercise to gain mutual understanding

Understanding the origins of current dynamics often proves valuable for resolving long-standing conflicts, deepening intimacy, and creating healthier relationship patterns.

Digging Into Your Shared Story: Relationship Archaeology

Ever notice how sometimes you and your partner get stuck in the same argument loop? Or how specific comments can trigger significant reactions that seem disproportionate? That's where relationship archaeology comes in!

Think of it as being relationship detectives together. Just like archaeologists carefully brush away dirt to reveal ancient treasures, you and your person can gently explore your shared history to uncover the hidden gems (and occasional fossils) that make your relationship unique.

It works like this: You look back at patterns in how you communicate, remember those early "lightbulb moments" when you connected, and explore why certain things might trigger one or both of you. The cool part is discovering those "Oh, THAT'S why we do that!" moments.

This isn't about blame or dwelling on past hurts. It's about understanding the unique language and history of your relationship. Maybe you realise your partner gets quiet during disagreements because that's how their family handles conflict. Or perhaps you discover that your sensitivity about career comments stems from something said years ago.

Some couples do this naturally through late-night conversations, while others might explore it with a therapist's guidance. Either way, it can transform frustrating patterns into opportunities for deeper connection.

The real magic happens when both people approach it with curiosity rather than criticism. After all, you're not just uncovering artefacts – you're discovering the beautiful, complicated story of how you became "us."

Understanding Your Attachment Style

Have you ever caught yourself thinking, "Why do I always end up with the same type of partner?" or "Why does this relationship feel eerily familiar to my last three breakups?" Welcome to the fascinating world of relationship archaeology, where we delve into the layers of your romantic history to uncover patterns you may not have even realized existed.

Think of me as your relationship Indiana Jones, minus the fedora and with significantly fewer booby traps (though your ex might disagree). Together, we're about to dust off your attachment style—that invisible blueprint that's been secretly directing your love life since before you could say, "It's not you; it's me."

The truth is, we're all walking around with emotional software that was installed during our childhood. This software—our attachment style—influences everything from how we choose partners to how we fight about whose turn it is to take out the trash. And the kicker? Most of us are unaware that it's running in the background.

Your attachment style is essentially your relationship operating system. It was developed through your earliest connections with carers, and it has quietly influenced your romantic choices ever since. Like that outdated phone suggesting you reconnect with people you've long blocked, your attachment patterns keep steering you toward familiar territory—even when that territory includes bright red flags that could guide ships to shore.

The good news? Unlike your genetic predisposition to your mother's nose or your father's receding hairline, attachment styles can be updated. Think of this chapter as your personal system upgrade—Relationship OS 2.0, if you will.

By uncovering your attachment style, you'll gain the superpower of self-awareness. You'll start to recognise when you're reacting based on old wounds rather than present circumstances. You'll catch yourself before sending that 2 AM text that seemed like a brilliant idea after three glasses of wine. You'll understand why certain behaviours from partners trigger you faster than a horror movie jump scare.

Over the following few pages, we'll explore the four main attachment styles:

Secure: The relationship unicorns who somehow communicate effectively and trust appropriately.

Anxious: The "are you mad at me?" crowd who check their phones every three minutes to see if their text has been read.

Avoidant: The emotional distancers who start planning their exit strategy before the first date has ended.

Disorganised: Those with a chaotic mix of anxious and avoidant tendencies who simultaneously fear abandonment and intimacy.

Don't worry if you recognise yourself in multiple categories—most of us aren't attachment purists. We're more like attachment smoothies, with a primary style and mixed dashes of the others.

So, grab your emotional shovel and dust brush. We're about to excavate some relationship artifacts that might explain why you've been stuck in patterns that make reruns of your favourite TV show seem less predictable. Remember, the goal isn't to judge your past relationships (or yourself) but to understand them—because understanding is the first step toward change.

And who knows? By the end of this archaeological expedition, you might discover that the treasure you've been searching for wasn't buried in someone else all along—it was hidden within yourself.

The Impact of Early Relationships on Partner Selection

Ever wonder why your friend keeps dating people who could be clones of their ex? Or why do you find yourself mysteriously drawn to partners who recreate familiar childhood dynamics? It's not a coincidence; you're not cursed—it's attachment theory in action.

Our earliest relationships—particularly with parents or primary caregivers—don't just fade into cute childhood memories. They become the invisible template for how we expect relationships to function. Think of it as your romantic GPS, constantly recalculating routes that lead back to familiar emotional territory, even when that territory resembles a psychological minefield.

If you grew up with a parent who was unpredictably available—sometimes attentive, sometimes distant—you might find yourself magnetically attracted to similarly unpredictable partners. Your brain recognises this emotional rollercoaster and thinks, "Ah, this feels like love!" Meanwhile, your friends watch in horror as you declare undying affection for someone who takes three days to respond to your text.

Or perhaps you had carers who require you to be perfect to receive love and approval. Is it any surprise you're now drawn to critical partners who make you feel like you're constantly auditioning for the role of "Good Enough"? Your attachment system is simply seeking what feels normal, not what feels good.

The real kicker? These patterns are mainly unconscious. You're not deliberately choosing partners who recreate your childhood drama—your attachment system is doing the casting without your knowledge.

Consider Sarah, who grew up with an emotionally distant father. Despite being intelligent and insightful in every other area of her life, she repeatedly found herself attracted to emotionally unavailable men. Each time, she believed this one would be different—this one would open up if she loved him enough. Her conscious mind sought connection, but her attachment system sought the familiar dance of pursuing someone just out of emotional reach.

Take Marcus, whose mother was overbearing and critical. He was drawn to controlling partners who dictated everything from his career choices to his wardrobe. While he complained about feeling smothered, part of him interpreted this behaviour as care—because that's what his early relationships taught him love looks like.

The good news? Awareness is the first step toward breaking these patterns. Once you understand how your early relationships shaped your partner-picking algorithm, you can start questioning its recommendations. That pull toward the charming but noncommittal guy at the bar. That's your attachment system running its old program. That inexplicable comfort with someone who subtly undermines your confidence. That's familiarity, not compatibility.

By recognising these patterns, you can begin making conscious choices rather than unconscious ones. You can learn to distinguish between the flutter of genuine connection and the flutter of familiar dysfunction. You can update your internal GPS to navigate toward healthier relationships, even if they initially feel foreign.

Remember, understanding your attachment patterns isn't about blaming your parents or past partners. It's about reclaiming your power to choose relationships based on what you truly want, not what feels unconsciously familiar. It's about writing a new relationship story rather than retelling the old one with different characters.

So the next time you feel that irresistible pull toward someone, ask yourself: Is this attraction based on possibility or pattern? Your answer might just save you from another archaeological dig through the ruins of a relationship built on old blueprints.

Identify Your Unique Relationship Patterns

You know that moment when you're watching a movie and suddenly think, "Wait, haven't I seen this plot before?" Many of us experience the same déjà vu in our love lives, starring in personal romantic reruns without realising we've repeatedly been cast in the same role. Let's roll up our sleeves and examine your relationship highlight reel to spot those recurring themes.

Grab a notebook (or open your notes app if pen and paper seem as outdated as a flip phone), and let's play relationship detective. Don't worry—unlike your last blind date, this exercise won't ghost you halfway through.

First, list your significant romantic relationships. For each one, jot down:

- How you met (the "cute" beginning)

- What initially attracted you to them

- Common conflicts or issues that emerged

- How you typically respond to problems

- How the relationship ended (if it did)

- Emotions you experienced throughout

Now, step back and look for the patterns. They might jump out like neon signs, or they might be subtle threads woven throughout your romantic history:

Do you see the same story with different characters? Perhaps you repeatedly fall for the "needs to be fixed" partner, the emotionally unavailable intellectual, or the free spirit who eventually feels constrained by commitment.

Notice your conflict patterns. Do you become the peacekeeper who swallows their needs? The explosive reactor, who makes sure their feelings are heard? The withdrawer who needs three days of silence before discussing issues?

Examine your relationship timelines. Do things follow a predictable arc? The three-month honeymoon phase was followed by the four-month power struggle, culminating in the inevitable six-month breakdown.

Consider your exit strategies. Do you typically end relationships at the first sign of trouble? Or do you hang on long past the expiration date, desperately trying to revive what's flatlined?

Take Sam, who realised all his relationships followed an eerily similar script: intense attraction to highly independent partners, initial bliss where he bent over backwards to accommodate their needs, growing resentment about their self-sufficiency, passive-aggressive attempts to make them more dependent, and finally, a dramatic breakup where he was accused of being controlling: different partners, same dance—every time.

Or consider Leila, who discovered her pattern of choosing emotionally unavailable partners wasn't random. She realized she was unconsciously selecting people who couldn't fully commit because, deep down, she feared true intimacy herself. Pursuing the unpersuadable, she maintained the illusion of wanting connection while ensuring it never happened.

These patterns aren't coincidences—they're clues. They reveal the attachment strategies you developed to navigate your earliest relationships, strategies that once helped you survive but may now sabotage your happiness.

The point isn't to judge yourself harshly or to reduce complex relationships to simple formulas. It's to recognise that you have more agency than you think. You're not doomed to repeat the same relationship story until the credits roll on your dating life.

By identifying your patterns, you gain the superpower of choice. The next time you feel that familiar pull toward a specific type of person or notice yourself slipping into old relationship dynamics, you can pause and ask: "Is this what I truly want, or is this just what feels familiar?"

Remember, the most crucial relationship pattern to identify isn't with others—it's with yourself. How do you treat yourself within relationships? What do you believe you deserve? What parts of yourself do you abandon to maintain a connection?

Because here's the truth: Your relationship with yourself sets the template for every other relationship in your life. Change that foundation, and you change everything built upon it.

Case Studies: These Common Types

Let's dive into some real-world relationship archetypes that might feel eerily familiar. Think of these as "greatest hits" from the attachment style playlist—characters you've likely met, dated, or perhaps even recognised in the mirror.

The Anxious Pursuer

Meet Alex: Always the first to text and the last to sleep, constantly checking for those three dots that indicate a response is coming. Alex's relationships begin with intense connections but quickly evolve into a quest for reassurance. After being left by a partner who "needed space," Alex developed a sixth sense for detecting potential abandonment—unfortunately, this radar frequently gives false positives.

Alex's phone is a battleground of drafted messages, deleted texts, and carefully timed responses, calculated not to appear too eager. Dates aren't enjoyed at the moment but are analysed afterwards for signs of waning interest. When a partner is distant, Alex becomes a detective, searching for evidence of betrayal or rejection.

Alex doesn't realise that this hypervigilance stems from a childhood where love felt conditional. Now, any hint of emotional distance triggers panic, creating the very distance Alex fears. Partners who initially appreciate Alex's attentiveness eventually feel suffocated, reinforcing Alex's belief that closeness can't last.

The Avoidant Distancer

Meet Jordan: Charming, independent, and mysteriously elusive. Jordan's relationships follow a pattern: intense attraction and sudden claustrophobia when things get serious. Jordan values self-sufficiency above all else and views emotional needs as weaknesses.

Jordan's apartment is a fortress of solitude with minimal evidence of a shared life. "Taking space" is Jordan's solution to every relationship problem. Discussions about the future are skilfully deflected with jokes or vague promises. When partners express hurt, Jordan feels irrationally annoyed—why can't they be cool?

Jordan doesn't realise that this pattern developed from early learning that depending on others leads to disappointment. Independence became Jordan's armour. The emotional intimacy Jordan avoids is precisely what Jordan secretly craves, but fears won't be reciprocated if vulnerabilities are exposed.

The Secure Base

Meet Sam: Refreshingly straightforward and emotionally available. Sam doesn't play games, responds to texts without calculating the "right" timing, and means it when asking, "How was your day?" Conflict doesn't trigger panic or shutdown—Sam approaches problems as "us versus the issue" rather than "me versus you."

Sam's relationships aren't perfect, but they're stable. There's room for both closeness and independence. Sam can express needs directly without fear and can hear a partner's complaints without feeling personally attacked.

What makes Sam different: Growing up with consistent caregiving created a foundation of essential trust. Sam learned that relationships could weather storms, needs can be expressed, and love doesn't disappear during conflicts. This security allows Sam to choose partners based on genuine compatibility rather than unconscious attachment triggers.

The Anxious-Avoidant Trap

Meet Taylor and Casey: Their relationship is the ultimate emotional rollercoaster. Taylor (anxious) craves closeness and reassurance, while Casey (avoidant) needs space and independence. They're magnetically drawn to each other despite—or because of—this fundamental mismatch.

Their cycle is predictable: Casey's emotional distance triggers Taylor's pursuit, which triggers Casey's withdrawal, which intensifies Taylor's anxiety. They break up regularly but reunite passionately, reinforcing their belief that this volcanic connection must be true love.

They don't realise that they're perfect attachment-style dance partners, each confirming the other's deepest relationship beliefs. Taylor's pursuit validates Casey's fear that relationships can be suffocating, while Casey's distance confirms Taylor's fear that love can be unreliable.

The People-Pleaser

Meet Riley, the perfect partner who somehow never seems to have their preferences. Want to see that movie? Sure! Do you prefer Thai food over Italian? Absolutely! Riley prides themselves on being easygoing but harbours resentment when partners don't reciprocate this accommodating nature.

Riley's relationships often end with partners complaining they never knew the "real" Riley, while Riley feels unappreciated for years of sacrifice. The painful irony: Riley gives and gives, hoping someone will finally recognise this devotion and spontaneously give back, but never directly asks for what's needed.

What Riley doesn't realise: This pattern stems from learning that love must be earned through performance and self-sacrifice. Riley doesn't understand that authentic connection requires showing up as your real self—with your preferences, needs, and flaws.

The Relationship Saboteur

Meet Morgan: Things are going great until they're not. When relationships reach a certain depth, Morgan finds flaws that suddenly seem intolerable or creates conflicts that conveniently end things before they get too serious. Morgan is confused about why things always fall apart "just when they were getting good."

Morgan's dating profile should honestly read: "Looking for perfection. Will flee when you reveal you're human." Friends have stopped getting invested in Morgan's relationships, knowing they have a predictable expiration date.

What Morgan doesn't realise is that this sabotage is a pre-emptive strike against anticipated pain. Morgan's attachment system believes that controlling when and how relationships end is safer than risking unexpected rejection or abandonment.

The Relationship Renovator

Meet Drew: A specialist in potential rather than reality. Drew repeatedly falls for people who could be perfect "if only" they would change in specific ways. These projects always seem promising at first—small victories fuel hope—but inevitably end in frustration when partners refuse to follow the renovation blueprint.

Drew's relationships are a series of improvement campaigns, with disappointment mounting as the gap between the ideal partner and the actual human being becomes undeniable.

What Drew doesn't realise: This pattern allows Drew to maintain the illusion of closeness while avoiding genuine intimacy. By focusing on changing the other person, Drew never has to be fully seen or known, keeping the relationship in a convenient state of "under construction."

Does any of this sound familiar? The first step toward healthier relationships isn't finding the perfect partner—it's recognising these patterns in yourself and understanding their origins. You can choose when you know better, breaking free from the unconscious scripts directing your love life behind the scenes.

Remember: These patterns developed for a reason. They once helped you navigate your earliest relationships. Be gentle with yourself as you work to update your attachment operating system—it's challenging work, but the possibility of secure, fulfilling connection is worth the upgrade.

Self-Assessment: Mapping Your Relationship History

Ready to play archaeologist with your own love life? This excavation might unearth some uncomfortable artefacts, but don't worry—we're digging for insight, not judgment. Grab some paper or open a fresh document because we're about to create the ultimate relationship timeline.

Step 1: Create Your Relationship Map

Draw a horizontal line across your page—this is your relationship timeline from your first significant connection to the present. Mark each major relationship along this line, including:

- First crushes and teenage relationships (yes, even that three-week high school drama)

- Serious long-term partnerships

- Brief but impactful connections

- "It's complicated" situations that never got a proper label

- Current relationships

For each relationship, note:

- When it began and ended

- How intense it felt (1-10 scale)

- How it ended (mutual decision, your choice, their choice, external circumstances)

- One word that captures how you felt during the relationship

- One word that describes how you felt after it ended

Step 2: Identify Your Patterns

Now, look at your map with detective's eyes. Search for recurring themes:

The Selection Pattern: What initially attracted you to each person? Look beyond physical traits to emotional qualities. Were you drawn to confidence? Vulnerability? Need? The emotionally unavailable? Those who needed saving?

The Honeymoon Pattern: How did your relationships typically begin? With passionate intensity? Cautious friendship first? Did you tend to merge quickly or maintain careful boundaries?

The Conflict Pattern: What issues kept resurfacing across different relationships? How were disagreements handled? Did you tend to avoid conflict, escalate it, or address it directly?

The Ending Pattern: Do your relationships tend to end for similar reasons? Do you usually initiate the breakup or get left? Do things typically end with drama, ghosting, or conscious uncoupling?

Step 3: Connect the Dots to Your Early Attachments

This is where things get interesting. Consider how your relationship patterns might connect to your earliest attachments:

If you consistently choose partners who need rescuing, did you have to be the responsible one in your family? Were you parentified or expected to care for others' emotional needs from a young age?

If you're attracted to the emotionally unavailable: Did you have caregivers who were physically present but emotionally distant? Did you learn that love means yearning rather than having?

If you panic when your partners need space: Did separation from caregivers feel threatening in your childhood? Were expressions of independence discouraged?

If you flee when relationships deepen, were you taught that self-reliance is the highest virtue? Did depending on others prove disappointing?

Step 4: Identify Your Attachment Triggers

What specific situations reliably activate your attachment system?

- Are they unanswered texts?

- Is a partner going out without you?

- Hearing "we need to talk"?

- Feeling criticised or inadequate?

- Is someone getting too close too quickly?

Understanding your triggers helps you distinguish between actual relationship threats and attachment echoes from your past.

Step 5: Recognize Your Protest Behaviours

When your attachment system is triggered, how do you typically respond?

- Do you become clingy and demand reassurance?

- Do you withdraw and create emotional distance?

- Do you pick fights to test the relationship?

- Do you try to make your partner jealous?

- Do you threaten to leave?

These "protest behaviours" are your attachment system's desperate attempts to restore connection or protect you from pain—but they often backfire, creating exactly what you fear.

Step 6: Write Your Relationship Story (Then Rewrite It)

Based on your observations, write a paragraph summarising your relationship patterns. This might look something like:

"I tend to be attracted to emotionally unavailable people who give me just enough attention to keep me interested but never fully commit. My relationships start intensely but cool when I express my needs. I try to be the perfect partner, hiding my true feelings until resentment builds, and I eventually explode or withdraw. Things usually end when I finally realise they'll never change, though I typically stay much longer than I should."

Now, write the relationship story you want to create going forward. This is your chance to author a new narrative:

"I want to be attracted to emotionally available partners who can meet me halfway. I want to express my needs clearly and choose people who respond positively. I want to be authentic rather than perfect, addressing issues as they arise instead of letting resentment build. I want to recognise incompatibility early rather than trying to change people."

Step 7: Compassionate Awareness

As you review your patterns, remember: These aren't character flaws—they're adaptation strategies. They developed for good reasons, helping you navigate your earliest relationships. Thank these patterns for trying to protect you, even as you work to update them.

The mere act of mapping your relationship history creates new awareness. With awareness comes choice, and with choice comes the possibility of different outcomes. You're not doomed to repeat patterns that no longer serve you. Each new relationship offers a fresh opportunity to write a different story—one where your past informs but doesn't dictate your future.

Remember, the goal isn't perfect attachment—it's conscious relationship choices that align with who you are and what you truly want. You've been operating from an unconscious script; now you're becoming the author of your own love story.

Research Spotlight: The Work of Dr. John Gottman on Relationship Patterns

If relationship research were an Olympic sport, Dr. John Gottman would be standing on the podium with more gold medals than Michael Phelps. After studying thousands of couples for over four decades, Gottman has developed an almost uncanny ability to predict relationship outcomes accurately.

The Love Lab Revolution

In the 1970s, Gottman established what couples affectionately (or nervously) call "The Love Lab" at the University of Washington. Unlike traditional therapeutic approaches that relied on self-reporting, Gottman hooked couples to devices measuring physiological responses while discussing issues in their relationships. Picture it: couples arguing about in-laws while scientists monitored their heart rates, sweat production, and blood pressure—reality TV before reality TV was cool.

The results were groundbreaking. Gottman discovered he could predict with over 90% accuracy which couples would divorce within a few years just by observing them interact for 15 minutes—no crystal ball needed—just science.

The Four Horsemen of the Relationship Apocalypse

Gottman's most famous contribution might be identifying what he dramatically termed "The Four Horsemen of the Apocalypse"—communication patterns that reliably predict relationship doom:

1. Criticism: Not to be confused with constructive feedback, criticism attacks a partner's character rather than addressing specific behaviours. "You never help with dishes" becomes "You're so lazy and selfish."

2. Contempt: The relationship killer supreme, contempt involves treating partners with disrespect, mockery, name-calling, eye-rolling, and hostile humour. It communicates disgust, and Gottman found it to be the single strongest predictor of divorce.

3. Defensiveness: When confronted, defensive partners deflect responsibility, make excuses, or counter-attack rather than acknowledge concerns. "I wouldn't have to yell if you would just listen!"

4. Stonewalling: When overwhelmed by negativity, some partners check out emotionally, withdrawing from interaction through silence, monosyllabic responses, or physically leaving. It's the conversational equivalent of installing a brick wall between you and your partner.

The Magic Relationship Ratio: 5:1

Gottman discovered that successful couples maintain a specific ratio of positive to negative interactions: 5:1. For every negative moment (a criticism, a complaint), stable relationships have five positive moments (a compliment, a touch, a laugh together).

This explains why some couples can fight like cats and dogs yet stay happily married—they've got enough positive deposits in their emotional bank account to weather withdrawals. Meanwhile, couples who maintain a more even ratio or, worse, more negative than positive interactions find themselves emotionally bankrupt.

Bids for Connection

One of Gottman's most applicable findings revolves around "bids for connection"—small attempts to gain attention, affection, or engagement. These might be as simple as saying, "Look at that beautiful bird!" or "How was your meeting today?"

The partner's response to these bids has a dramatic impact on relationship health. They can:

- **Turn toward**: Acknowledging the bid with interest ("Wow, that is a pretty bird!")

- **Turn away**: Ignoring the bid completely

- **Turn against**: Responding with hostility ("I'm trying to read. Stop interrupting me!")

Couples who "turned toward" each other's bids about 86% of the time stayed married, while those who divorced averaged only 33%. Small moments, it turns out, matter enormously.

Relationship Masters vs. Disasters

Through his research, Gottman identified two types of couples: "Masters" and "Disasters."

The Masters:

- Stay physiologically calmer during conflicts
- Take responsibility for their part in problems
- Accept influence from each other
- Make and receive repair attempts during arguments
- Focus on friendship and positivity

The Disasters:

- Experience flooding (overwhelming physiological arousal) during conflicts
- Get stuck in negative attributions about their partners
- Reject influence, especially men rejecting influence from women
- Miss or reject repair attempts during arguments
- Allow negativity to dominate their interactions

Practical Applications

Gottman's work stands out because it translates complex research into actionable strategies:

Create Shared Meaning: Successful couples develop shared goals, values, and symbols—a relationship culture that strengthens their bond.

Build Love Maps: Partners who remain curious about each other's worlds, regularly updating their mental maps of their partner's likes, dislikes, dreams, and concerns, maintain stronger connections.

Practice Physiological Self-Soothing: Recognizing when you're physiologically flooded (typically at heart rates above 100 bpm) and taking a 20-30 minute break before continuing difficult conversations.

Make Deposits in the Emotional Bank Account: Consciously increasing positive interactions, especially during conflict-free times.

Learn to Make and Receive Repair Attempts: Develop phrases and gestures that de-escalate tension during arguments.

Why Gottman's Work Matters

Unlike approaches focused primarily on communication skills, Gottman's research emphasises that lasting relationships depend on deep friendship, shared humour, and emotional connection—not just conflict management.

His work offers hope by demonstrating that relationship success isn't magical or mysterious—it's predictable and learnable. The patterns that predict divorce can be identified and changed before relationship damage becomes irreparable.

So, next time you find yourself eye-rolling at your partner or building a mental case for why you're right and they're wrong, remember: Gottman is watching (metaphorically), and science has some suggestions for a better approach. Your relationship future isn't written in stone—it's written in daily interactions that can change once you recognise the patterns.

CHAPTER 2:

The Attraction Trap

Why We're Drawn to the Wrong People

Have you ever looked at your dating history and thought, "What is WRONG with me?" Perhaps you've created a spreadsheet (just me?) to track the eerily similar ways your last five relationships imploded. Or maybe you've had that mortifying moment when you introduce someone new to your friends, only for them to pull you aside later and whisper, "So.. you're dating your ex again, but with different hair?"

Why We're All Members of the "What's Wrong With Me?" Club

Let's be honest: asking "What's wrong with me?" after relationship troubles is like trying to fix a computer by hitting it repeatedly—satisfying in the moment but rarely producing useful results.

This question typically appears in our internal monologue when:

- Your situationship just ended with a text that said
- Your date ghosted faster than a paranormal activity

- Your partner gave you that look when you explained why buying a pet alligator would solve all your problems

- You've recreated the same relationship dynamic so many times you could sell tickets to the show

It's a question that feels profound but leads us down a rabbit hole lined with self-criticism, misplaced blame, and occasionally ice cream at 3 AM. It's not your fault. Please remember that.

Better Questions That Won't Make Your Therapist Sigh

Instead of the self-flagellating classic "What's wrong with me?", try these more productive questions that won't have your friends secretly checking their battery life when you call. And if you think it's me writing from experience, no, ok, it's me.

1. what patterns do I notice?

Look for the reruns in your relationship history. If you've dated three people who consider texting back within the same week "moving too fast," that's valuable data!

2. What was my role in this dynamic?

Not to assign blame but to recognise your contribution to the relationship tango. Sometimes, you've been accidentally stepping on toes while insisting you're an excellent dancer.

3. "What needs wasn't this relationship meeting?"

Maybe you need someone who understands your obscure movie references. Or someone who doesn't think "emotional support" means patting you awkwardly on the head once a year.

4. "What did I learn that I can take forward?"

Every relationship—even the ones that end with you dramatically deleting all your social media and considering a move to Finland—teaches us something valuable.

5. "What am I feeling right now?"

Often, "What's wrong with me?" is just a disguise for "I feel rejected/hurt/disappointed/confused/like I want to eat an entire chocolate cake by myself."

The Healthy Relationship with Yourself Checklist

Before you fall down the "What's wrong with me?" hole again, run through this quick checklist:

- **Am I treating myself with the same kindness I'd show a friend?** If your best friend came to you feeling bad about a relationship, would you start listing all their flaws? No, because that would make you a terrible friend deserving of bad Wi-Fi forever.

- **Am I confusing a relationship mismatch with personal deficiency?** Not every lock works with every key, and not everyone who isn't right for you thinks you're a walking disaster. Sometimes it's just about fit.

- **Am I giving too much power to one person's opinion?** Remember: someone not appreciating your extensive knowledge of dinosaur facts doesn't mean dinosaur facts aren't excellent.

- **Am I romanticising my ex while catastrophising myself?** They weren't a flawless demigod, and you weren't a swamp creature. You were two imperfect humans doing your best.

- **Am I truly upset about this relationship, or am I revisiting past hurts?** Sometimes, our reaction is 10% about the current situation and 90% about that time in eighth grade when no one wanted to be our lab partner.

Don't worry; you're not crazy. Or if you are, we all are.

The truth about attraction is simultaneously fascinating and maddening: the very system designed to help us find suitable partners is often the same system steering us straight into relationship disaster. It's like having a GPS that consistently directs you to drive into lakes while cheerfully announcing, "You have arrived at your destination!"

So why does this happen? Why do smart, accomplished, otherwise sensible people repeatedly find themselves drawn to partners who are emotionally unavailable, commitment-phobic, or come with more red flags than a slalom skiing course?

Let's dive into the science of misguided attraction.

Your Brain on Familiarity: The Comfort of the Known

An inconvenient truth has derailed many a dating life: our brains are fundamentally wired to find comfort in the familiar, even when the familiar is uncomfortable.

Neuroscientists have found that our earliest relationship experiences—primarily with caregivers—create neural pathways that become our default templates for "what love feels like." These templates form what scientists call our "love map;" they're shockingly resistant to logical override.

If you grew up with inconsistent attention from caregivers (sometimes there, sometimes not), your brain may have learned that love and uncertainty often go hand-in-hand. Fast forward to adulthood, and you might find yourself magnetically drawn to partners who are inconsistent, while the consistently attentive potential partner seems "boring" or "there must be something wrong with them."

The Neurochemistry of Unhealthy Attraction

Picture this: You meet someone who sends your heart racing. They're gorgeous, charismatic, and just distant enough to keep you wondering where you stand. Three weeks in, you're checking your phone every five minutes, cancelling plans with friends to be available "just in case," and experiencing wild mood swings based on their inconsistent attention. Your friends are concerned. Your therapist is giving you That Look. Yet you can't help but think about them.

"I've never felt this way before," you tell anyone who'll listen. "It must be special."

Plot twist: It's not special. It's chemistry—and not the good kind.

What you're experiencing is your brain on relationship crack. Let me explain what's happening behind the scenes of that intoxicating attraction to someone who's probably terrible for you.

Your Brain's Drug Dealer: Meet the Reward System

Your brain contains a built-in reward system that has evolved to ensure the survival of the human species. When you engage in activities beneficial to survival—eating, sex, social bonding—your brain releases chemical messengers that make you feel good, essentially training you to repeat these behaviours.

This system was perfect for our ancestral environment. The problem? It wasn't designed for dating apps, situationships, or that person who texts you "good morning beautiful" daily but somehow never makes actual plans to see you.

Dopamine: The Chemical Culprit Behind "I Can't Stop Thinking About Them"

Dopamine is both a neurotransmitter (chemical messenger) and a hormone that plays a starring role in your brain's reward system. It's associated with pleasure, motivation, and anticipation. When something good or exciting happens—or might happen—dopamine floods your system.

Here's the neurochemical plot twist: dopamine spikes higher in conditions of unpredictability than consistency.

Let me repeat that: Your brain releases MORE dopamine when rewards are inconsistent and unpredictable than when they're reliable and consistent.

This is exactly why slot machines are so addictive. Every pull might be the big win! It's also why that person who sometimes replies instantly and sometimes ghosts you for days has you constantly checking your phone like it's dispensing oxygen.

That emotional rollercoaster you're riding? It's a dopamine carnival. The uncertainty of when you'll get your next "fix" of their attention keeps your brain in a state of hyperarousal and anticipation. Your brain isn't distinguishing between excitement and anxiety—it's just keeping you hooked on the possibility.

Oxytocin: The Attachment Accelerator

While dopamine keeps you hooked on the chase, oxytocin—often referred to as the "love hormone" or "bonding hormone"—is busy creating emotional attachment, even to people who treat you like a backup plan.

Oxytocin levels increase during physical touch (especially during sex), eye contact, and positive social interactions. It promotes feelings of trust, bonding, and emotional connection. This is beautiful when you're bonding with someone worthy of your trust. It's problematic when it creates an attachment to someone who has just breadcrumb their way into your life.

Here's the kicker: women typically produce more oxytocin than men, which may partially explain why women sometimes feel more attached after physical intimacy. Your body doesn't know your casual hookup isn't relationship material—it's busy creating biochemical bonds regardless of their emotional availability.

Cortisol: The Stress Hormone That Keeps You Coming Back

You'd think that stress would drive you away from someone, but in the twisted neurobiology of unhealthy attraction, even negative emotions can reinforce attachment.

Cortisol, your body's primary stress hormone, increases during states of uncertainty and anxiety-like when you're waiting for a text back or trying to interpret what "let's play it by ear" actually means for your Saturday night plans.

When cortisol levels rise and then fall (after they finally respond to you), you experience relief. This relief feels rewarding, but it creates another unhealthy cycle. Your brain starts associating the stress-relief pattern with the person, strengthening neural pathways that keep you addicted to the dynamic.

This explains why making up after a fight can feel so good and why tumultuous relationships can be so hard to leave despite being objectively terrible. You become addicted not just to the person but to the dramatic cortisol-dopamine roller coaster they provide.

Adrenaline: Mistaking Fear for Love

Do you remember the butterflies in your stomach when you're around someone new? That's partly adrenaline, which triggers your body's fight-or-flight response. Adrenaline increases heart rate, heightens senses, and creates that feeling of excitement.

The problem? Your body produces similar physical responses to both fear and attraction. This biological confusion is why bungee jumping on a first date is a terrible idea (unless you want to attribute your normal fear response to romantic chemistry mistakenly).

It also explains why slightly intimidating, unpredictable people can seem more attractive than stable, reliable ones. Your brain misinterprets the adrenaline rush as an intense attraction rather than recognising it as your nervous system's warning signal.

Breaking the Chemical Addiction to Unhealthy Relationships

Understanding the neurochemistry of unhealthy attraction is the first step toward making better relationship choices. Knowledge doesn't automatically change behaviour, but it gives you a different perspective when your brain tries to convince you that emotional unavailability is exciting.

The next time you find yourself obsessing over someone who treats connection like an optional hobby, remember: That feeling isn't unique cosmic chemistry—it's your brain's reward system being hijacked. You're not experiencing a once-in-a-lifetime passion; you're experiencing the same neurobiological response that slot machines are specifically designed to trigger.

Healthy love should feel good, unlike withdrawal from a substance you can't quit. It should bring peace, not persistent anxiety. And while the early stages of any connection involve some uncertainty, someone worth your time will attempt to minimise your doubts, not strategically maintain them to keep you hooked.

Your brain may be wired to chase unpredictable rewards, but your life is too valuable to spend it waiting for emotional crumbs from someone treating you like an option. The most powerful neurotransmitter you have access to is your frontal lobe's ability to recognise patterns and make different choices—use it.

Red Flags vs. Green Flags: A Complete Guide

Let's talk about flags. No, not the kind you plant on a mountain summit or wave at a parade. I'm talking about relationship flags—those signals and behaviours that can tell you whether you're headed toward relationship bliss or a Netflix documentary where friends sadly recall how they "never saw it coming."

Understanding the difference between red flags (warning signs) and green flags (positive indicators) is like having a relationship with GPS. But unlike the GPS on your phone, this one actually tells you when you're about to drive off a cliff.

What Are Relationship Flags?

Let's get clear on what we're talking about:

Red flags are warning signs—behaviours, values, or patterns that indicate potential problems ahead. They don't always mean "run for the hills," but they do mean "pay attention."

Green flags are positive indicators—behaviours, values, or patterns that suggest someone could be a healthy partner. They're not guarantees of compatibility, but they're good signs that basic relationship ingredients are present.

Both types of flags exist on a spectrum of options. Some red flags are mild caution signs (they leave their dishes in the sink), while others are stop-the-car-and-get-out emergencies (they casually mention their restraining orders in plural form). Similarly, green flags range from basic human decency (respects your boundaries) to the relatively rare (has done meaningful work in therapy).

Now, let's explore these flags across different dimensions of relationships.

Communication Flags

Red Flags in Communication:

- **Conversational Narcissism:** Every topic somehow boomerangs back to them. You mention your promotion, and they launch into a 20-minute story about their career trajectory. You say your sick grandmother, and they tell you about how they once felt ill at their grandmother's house.

- **Chronic Interrupting:** They can't let you finish a thought without jumping in. This indicates they're forming their response rather than listening to understand you.

- **Communication Shutdown:** They refuse to discuss certain topics or respond with "whatever" or "I don't care" when you bring up concerns.

- **Weaponized Incompetence:** "I'm just not good at talking about feelings" becomes an excuse to never develop emotional communication skills.

- **Hostile Communication:** Name-calling, mocking, sarcasm, or contempt during disagreements.

- **Silent Treatment:** Using silence as punishment rather than taking space to cool down.

- **Conversation Avoidance:** They change the subject when anything meaningful or potentially uncomfortable comes up.

- **Gaslighting:** Denying your reality or making you question your own perceptions and memories.

Green Flags in Communication:

- **Active Listening:** They ask follow-up questions and reference things you've told them previously.

- **Healthy Conflict Skills:** They can discuss disagreements without attacking your character or shutting down.

- **Appropriate Self-Disclosure:** They gradually share meaningful information about themselves, neither oversharing trauma on the first date nor remaining a mystery six months in.

- **Curiosity About You:** They show genuine interest in your thoughts, feelings, and experiences.

- **Accountability Language:** They use "I" statements and take responsibility for their actions and feelings.

- **Receptiveness to Feedback:** When you express a concern, they consider it seriously rather than becoming defensive.

- **Respects Communication Boundaries:** They understand when it's appropriate to have certain conversations (not bringing up relationship issues at your grandmother's funeral, for instance).

Emotional Intelligence Flags

Red Flags in Emotional Intelligence:

- **Limited Emotional Vocabulary:** Everything is either "fine" or "not fine" with no nuance.

- **Emotional Dysregulation:** Disproportionate emotional reactions to minor frustrations.

- **Inability to Identify Emotions:** They don't recognize what they're feeling or why.

- **Emotional Bypassing:** They dismiss feelings with toxic positivity ("just think happy thoughts!").

- **Emotional Dumping:** They offload all their feelings onto you without reciprocity or boundaries.

- **Emotional Weaponization:** They use your emotional reactions against you ("See how crazy you get?").

- **Lacks Empathy:** They show indifference to others' suffering or find it annoying when others express emotions.

Green Flags in Emotional Intelligence:

- **Emotional Self-Awareness:** They can identify and articulate their feelings.

- **Emotional Self-Regulation:** They can experience strong emotions without being controlled by them.

- **Empathy:** They genuinely care about others' emotional experiences.

- **Emotional Accountability:** They don't blame others for their feelings.

- **Emotional Generosity:** They make room for your emotions even when inconvenient.

- **Comfortable With Vulnerability:** They can share authentic feelings without manipulation.

- **Emotional Boundaries:** They take responsibility for their emotions while respecting yours.

Respect Flags

Red Flags in Respect:

- **Boundary Violations:** They push past your clearly stated limits, from minor ("I said I'm not ready to meet your parents") to major ("I said I don't want to sleep together yet").

- **"Respect" Based on Fear:** They mistake intimidation for respect.

- **Disrespect Toward Others:** They're rude to service workers, dismissive of people they deem "unimportant," or talk down to others.

- **Double Standards:** Rules for you don't apply to them.

- **Punishing Independence:** They sulk, withdraw, or become hostile when you pursue your own interests or spend time with others.

- **Contempt:** They roll their eyes, mock you, or speak to you with disdain.

- **Privacy Violations:** They go through your phone, read your messages, or demand access to your accounts.

Green Flags in Respect:

- **Honors Boundaries:** They accept your "no" without punishment or pressure.

- **Respects Your Time:** They value your schedule and commitments.

- **Digital Respect:** They ask before posting photos of you or sharing your personal information.

- **Respects Your Relationships:** They speak well of people important to you and support those connections.

- **Respects Your Autonomy:** They recognize your right to make your own decisions, even when they disagree.

- **Treats Others With Dignity:** They're courteous to everyone, not just people they want to impress.

- **Respects Differences:** They can disagree with you without trying to change your mind.

Trust Flags

Red Flags in Trust:

- **Jealousy as Love:** They frame controlling behaviour as evidence of caring.

- **Unwarranted Accusations:** They frequently suspect you of lying or cheating without cause.

- **History of Infidelity:** They've cheated in past relationships and show no insight into why.

- **Secrecy About Basic Information:** They're mysteriously unavailable at certain times or vague about their whereabouts.

- **Inconsistency:** Their words and actions rarely align.

- **Testing Behaviours:** They set up "tests" to see if you'll cheat or lie.

- **Selective Truth-Telling:** They tell half-truths or lie by omission.

Green Flags in Trust:

- **Reliability:** They do what they say they'll do.

- **Consistency:** Their behaviour is predictable in healthy ways.

- **Appropriate Transparency:** They share information relevant to the relationship stage.

- **Trustworthiness:** They keep your confidence and respect your privacy.

- **Self-Trust:** They trust their judgment and don't require constant reassurance.

- **Extends Trust to You:** They don't demand proof of your whereabouts or activities.

- **Trusts the Relationship:** They believe in the connection between you.

Independence/Interdependence Flags

Red Flags in Independence/Interdependence:

- **Instant Relationship Fusion:** They want to spend every moment together from the very first week.

- **Isolation Tactics:** They gradually separate you from friends and family.

- **Identity Absorption:** They adopt your interests, style, or beliefs wholesale.

- **Pathological Independence:** They're unwilling to depend on anyone for anything.

- **Scorekeeping:** They track every favour or contribution to ensure absolute equality.

- **Controlling Finances:** They restrict your access to money or monitor all spending.

- **Separation Anxiety:** They become distressed when you're apart for regular periods.

Green Flags in Independence/Interdependence:

- **Healthy Attachments Outside the Relationship:** They maintain friendships and family connections.

- **Support for Your Independence:** They encourage your individual growth and interests.

- **Secure Attachment:** They can be apart from you without anxiety.

- **Interdependence Without Co-Dependency: They value connection without relying on others** for their sense of self.

- **Financial Clarity:** They're transparent about money without being controlling.

- **Shared Decision-Making:** They consider your input on matters that affect both of you.

- **Social Integration:** They welcome integrating friend groups and family connections at appropriate times.

Conflict Resolution Flags

Red Flags in Conflict Resolution:

- **Stonewalling:** They shut down or give you the silent treatment during disagreements.

- **Physical Intimidation:** They use their body, voice, or actions to frighten you during conflicts.

- **Bringing Up the Past:** They resurrect old issues to avoid addressing current problems.

- **Win-at-All-Costs Mentality:** The goal is victory, not resolution.

- **Conflict Avoidance:** They refuse to acknowledge problems until they become unmanageable.

- **Name-calling or Degradation:** They attack your character rather than addressing the issue.

- **Post-Conflict Punishment:** They withhold affection or connection after disagreements.

Green Flags in Conflict Resolution:

- **Repair Attempts:** They make efforts to de-escalate tension during disagreements.

- **Focus on Understanding:** They strive to see your perspective before defending their own.

- **Solution-oriented:** They work toward resolution rather than being right.

- **Takes Timeouts When Needed:** They recognise when emotions are too high and suggest breaks.

- **Conflict Without Contempt:** They can disagree without disrespecting you.

- **Apologizes Sincerely:** They take responsibility for their part in problems.

- **Post-Conflict Reconnection:** They make efforts to rebuild connections after disagreements.

Personal Growth Flags

Red Flags in Personal Growth:

- **Rigid Thinking:** They're unwilling to consider new perspectives or ideas.

- **Perpetual Victim Mentality:** They believe that nothing is ever their responsibility.

- **Stagnation:** They've experienced no growth or significant changes in key areas of life for years.

- **Resistance to Self-Improvement:** They view personal development as unnecessary or threatening.

- **Idealization of the Past:** They constantly reference "the good old days" as superior.

- **Addiction Without Recovery:** They have untreated substance issues or behavioural addictions.

- **Unresolved Trauma:** They have significant unaddressed wounds affecting their functioning.

Green Flags in Personal Growth:

- **Self-Reflection Capacity:** They think about their patterns and behaviours.

- **Humility:** They can admit mistakes and see their limitations.

- **Growth Mindset:** They believe that people, including themselves, can change and develop.

- **Investment in Learning:** They strive to gain a deeper understanding of themselves and the world.

- **Healthy Relationship with Therapy:** They view therapeutic help as valuable, whether or not they're currently in therapy.

- **Constructive Self-Criticism:** They can honestly assess themselves without shame spirals.

- **Values Clarification:** They've thought about what matters to them and why.

Practical Living Flags

Red Flags in Practical Living:

- **Financial Chaos:** Extreme debt, gambling issues, or complete financial disorganisation without a plan.

- **Basic Skills Deficit:** They are unable to perform age-appropriate life tasks, such as cooking simple meals, doing laundry, and basic budgeting.

- **Chronic Joblessness:** They struggle to maintain employment without valid reasons.

- **Substance Dependence:** Their daily functioning requires alcohol or drugs.

- **Living Space Neglect:** Their home is unhygienic beyond everyday messiness.

- **Legal Problems:** Ongoing issues with the law that they don't take seriously.

- **Digital Life Dominance:** Screen time that interferes with basic functioning or relationships.

Green Flags in Practical Living:

- **Financial Responsibility:** They live within their means and have financial goals.

- **Home Management Skills:** They can maintain a reasonably functional living space.

- **Work Ethic:** They take their professional responsibilities seriously.

- **Healthy Habits:** They make efforts to care for their physical health.

- **Time Management:** They can generally balance various life demands.

- **Problem-solving skills:** They can handle everyday challenges without crisis.

- **Digital Boundaries:** They can put down their phone and be present.

Inner Circle Flags

Red Flags in Their Inner Circle:

- **No Long-term Friends:** They have no sustained relationships in their life.

- **Everyone Else is "Crazy":** All their exes, former friends, and estranged family members are painted as villains.

- **Friend Group Red Flags:** Their close friends exhibit concerning behaviours they excuse or minimise.

- **Social Isolation:** They have no meaningful connections outside of romantic relationships.

- **Inappropriate Boundaries:** Their relationships with friends or family members seem concerning or uncomfortable.

- **Relationship Privacy Violations:** They share intimate details of your relationship with others without your consent.

- **Us-Against-the-World Mentality:** They frame outside relationships as threats to your bond.

Green Flags in Their Inner Circle:

- **Healthy Friendships:** They maintain positive, reciprocal friendships.

- **Speaks Respectfully of Exes:** They acknowledge their role in past relationship dynamics.

- **Family Self-Awareness:** They have appropriate boundaries with family, whether close or distant.

- **Relationship Integration:** They introduce you to important people in their lives at appropriate times.

- **Friend Quality:** The people they choose to have in their lives are kind, supportive individuals.

- **Balanced Loyalties:** They can be dedicated to you while maintaining other vital connections.

- **Relationship Privacy:** They respect the privacy of your relationship without keeping it a secret.

Relationship Experience Flags

Red Flags in Relationship Experience:

- **Perpetual Honeymoon Seeker:** They have multiple short relationships that never develop depth.

- **Immediate Intensity:** They fall in love within days and want an instant commitment.

- **Unhealed Wounds:** They remain actively hostile towards or obsessed with their ex-partners.

- **Relationship Gap Denial:** They claim their 7-year absence from dating was due to "no one meeting their standards."

- **Instant Relationship Expert:** Despite limited experience, they're confident they know precisely how relationships should work.

- **Refuses to Discuss Past:** They shut down all conversations about previous relationships.

- **Relationship Identity Crisis:** They become entirely different people with each new partner.

Green Flags in Relationship Experience:

- **Reflective About Past Relationships:** They can identify patterns and lessons from previous experiences.

- **Appropriate Relationship Pace:** They allow connection to develop naturally without forcing intimacy.

- **Healing Period:** They've taken time between significant relationships to process and grow.

- **Responsibility in Breakups:** They acknowledge their contributions to past relationship endings.

- **Experience Integration:** They've applied insights from past relationships to personal growth.

- **Relationship Learning Curve:** They recognise that relating skills develop over time.

- **Balanced Perspective:** They don't idealise or demonise past partners or relationships.

Value Alignment Flags

Red Flags in Value Alignment:

- **Fundamental Value Conflicts:** They want five kids while you want none; they believe in traditional gender roles while you don't.

- **Values Chameleon:** Their core values seem to shift depending on who they're with.

- **Dealbreaker Denial:** They dismiss significant value differences as "details we can work out later."

- **Attempted Value Conversion:** They try to change your deeply held beliefs or values.

- **Political/Religious Extremism:** They hold rigid ideological positions that dehumanize others.

- **Incompatible Financial Values:** They're a spender, while you're a saver, or they believe in joint finances, whereas you value financial independence.

- **Different Definitions of Fidelity:** They consider certain behaviours acceptable that you view as cheating.

Green Flags in Value Alignment:

- **Core Value Compatibility:** You share similar views on key life values, such as family, money, and lifestyle.

- **Respect for Differences:** They can honour your different perspectives without trying to change them.

- **Similar Relationship Goals:** You want the same kind of partnership (monogamous, open, marriage, living separately, etc.).

- **Alignment on Major Life Decisions:** You have compatible views on children, location, and career priorities.

- **Communication About Values:** They can discuss values openly without judgment.

- **Ethical Consistency:** Their stated values match their actual behaviours.

- **Growth-Compatible Values:** Your growth directions seem complementary rather than conflicting.

Flag Interpretation Guidelines

1. **Context Matters:** A red flag in one context might be neutral in another. Someone living with parents at 35 might be a red flag—unless they're caring for an ill family member or rebuilding after a major setback.

2. **Patterns Over Incidents:** Everyone has bad days or makes mistakes. Look for repeated behaviours rather than isolated events.

3. **Flag Clustering:** Pay special attention when multiple red flags appear in the same category.

4. **Evolution Over Time:** Green flags should become more numerous as a healthy relationship develops.

5. **Trust Your Gut:** If something feels wrong, even if it seems minor, it's worth exploring further.

6. **Cultural Lens Awareness:** What constitutes a red or green flag may vary across cultures.

7. **Dealbreakers vs. Growth Areas:** Distinguish between flags that signal fundamental incompatibility and those that indicate areas for potential growth.

Final Thoughts: Your Personal Flag System

The most important relationship skill isn't finding someone with all green flags—it's knowing which flags matter most to YOU.

Your unique history, values, and needs mean certain flags carry more weight in your relationships. Someone with anxiety might prioritise a partner who shows the green flag of patience during stress responses. Someone with financial trauma might consider monetary secrecy an absolute dealbreaker.

Take time to develop your personal flag system. Which green flags do you need for security and happiness? Which red flags trigger your particular wounds? Which yellow flags could become green with communication and growth?

Remember: Flags aren't about judging someone's worth as a person. They're about assessing compatibility and potential for a healthy relationship between two specific people—you and them.

The right relationship won't be flag-free, but it will feature green flags in the areas most crucial to your well-being and red flags that you can navigate together rather than suffer through alone.

Breaking the Chemistry Addiction

Ah, chemistry. That intoxicating rush that makes you text your friends at 2 AM: "I've never felt this way before!" That feeling prompts you to create Spotify playlists titled "Finally Found You" after just one coffee date. That sensation that convinces you this time is different, even though this person checks all the same boxes as your last three relationship disasters.

If you've realised your version of chemistry has been leading you straight into relationship Chornobyl, you're probably wondering: Can I change what I'm attracted to? Or am I doomed to confuse emotional rollercoasters with romance forever?

The good news is that your attraction patterns can change. The less good news is that it won't happen through wishful thinking, pep talks from friends, or swiping right on different profile pictures. Breaking chemistry addiction requires a deliberate rewiring process.

Let's talk about how to break the cycle.

Step 1: Decode Your Chemistry Pattern

Before you can change your attraction pattern, you need to understand exactly what triggers that "chemistry" feeling for you. Grab a notebook and answer these questions:

- **Who were your last three intense "chemistry" connections?** (Include situationships, not just official relationships)

- **What qualities did these people share?** (Look beyond physical traits to emotional availability, communication style, and relationship patterns)

- **How did these connections make you feel?** (Both the highs AND the lows)

- **What childhood dynamics do these relationships evoke for you?** (This is where the real gold lies)

Most of us are unconsciously drawn to people who allow us to relive familiar emotional experiences from our childhood. If you grew up with an emotionally inconsistent parent, the unpredictable person who texts you "Good morning beautiful" for five days and then disappears for two might feel inexplicably magnetic. Your conscious mind says, "I want someone reliable," but your attachment system says, "THIS feels like home."

Step 2: Recognize Chemistry vs. Compatibility

Many people mistake intensity chemistry for intimacy. Let's clarify the difference:

Chemistry is:
- Instant
- Based primarily on unconscious triggers
- Often feels like a "high."
- Frequently involves anxiety and excitement
- Can exist without trust or compatibility

Compatibility is:
- Often builds gradually
- Based on shared values and goals
- Feels like peace and safety
- Involves comfort and calm
- Requires trust and mutual respect

Write down what both chemistry and compatibility would look like specifically for you. This mental clarity helps you recognise the difference when dating.

Step 3: Implement the Attraction Intervention

Now comes the active rewiring part. This is a multi-pronged approach:

The Two-Date Rule

If you're consistently attracted to relationship disaster zones, your initial attraction compass needs recalibration. Implement this rule: **Go on at least two dates with people you're not immediately drawn to**, assuming they're kind and respectful and you don't actively dislike them.

This isn't about settling—it's about giving your brain time to recognise attraction patterns that aren't based on unhealthy chemistry. Many people discover attraction grows when they're not distracted by the fireworks of dysfunctional chemistry.

The Feeling Inventory

After dates or new connections, complete this quick inventory:

- How did my body feel during our interaction? (Tense? Relaxed? Anxious? Calm?)

- Did I feel like my authentic self or like I was putting on a performance?

- Am I worried about what they're thinking about me right now?

- Do I feel peaceful or slightly obsessive?

These questions help you distinguish between healthy attraction and unhealthy activation of your attachment system.

The Slow Burn Experiment

Challenge yourself to date someone for 3 months where the connection builds gradually rather than explosively. This gives your brain time to develop new neural pathways that associate romance with consistency rather than chaos.

Many people discover that slow-burn relationships eventually create a more profound, more sustainable attraction—like building a fire from kindling rather than throwing a match on gasoline.

Step 4: Install New Attraction Software

Your current attraction settings were programmed through repeated experiences. Reprogramming requires the same approach:

Conscious Exposure Therapy

Deliberately expose yourself to examples of healthy love:

- Spend time with couples who have respectful, kind relationships
- Read books or watch shows featuring healthy relationships (they exist, though they're less dramatic)
- Create a "relationship values" playlist with songs about supportive, kind love

Attraction Journaling

Keep a daily log of moments when you feel attracted to healthier relationship dynamics. Perhaps you've noticed how your friend's partner remembers details about her day or how a couple at the coffee shop speaks respectfully, even during disagreements.

Actively looking for and noting these moments trains your brain to register these behaviours as attractive.

Visualisation Practice

Spend 5 minutes daily visualising yourself in a relationship with the qualities you rationally want. Feel the emotions of security, respect, and calm connection. This creates neural pathways that associate these feelings with romance.

Step 5: Manage the Withdrawal Period

When you start avoiding unhealthy chemistry connections, expect withdrawal symptoms. Your brain has been conditioned to associate romantic excitement with the dopamine rush of uncertainty. Breaking this association will trigger discomfort:

Withdrawal Symptoms May Include:

- Boredom with healthier connections
- Nostalgia for toxic past relationships
- Doubting if you can feel "passion" in healthy relationships
- Urges to text problematic exes
- Fantasies about the "one that got away"

Withdrawal Management Techniques:

- Name it to tame it: "This is withdrawal, not truth."
- Create a list of painful outcomes from past chemistry-driven relationships to review when nostalgia hits

- Establish a "withdrawal buddy" who will talk you through the urges

- Use physical activity to manage the physiological aspects of craving

Step 6: Celebrate New Patterns

Your brain needs evidence that new patterns lead to rewards:

- Notice and celebrate moments of healthy attraction

- Acknowledge the peace that comes from not being on an emotional rollercoaster

- Recognize the energy you now have for other areas of your life

- Appreciate the subtle joys of growing trust and safety

Real Talk: Timeline and Expectations

Changing attraction patterns isn't a weekend project—it's more like learning a new language. Expect:

- **1-3 months:** Heightened awareness of your patterns, but still feeling pulled toward old types

- **3-6 months:** Beginning to notice new types of people, with occasional strong pulls toward familiar patterns

- **6-12 months:** Genuinely finding new qualities attractive, with old patterns feeling less compelling

- **1 year+:** New attraction patterns feeling natural, with occasional need for conscious redirection

The process isn't linear. You'll have setbacks—moments where the familiar pull of unhealthy chemistry feels overwhelming. This doesn't mean you've failed; it means you're rewiring decades of programming. Be patient with yourself.

The Secret Most People Miss

Here's the truth most advice columns don't tell you: The most potent factor in changing your attraction patterns isn't who you date—it's how you relate to yourself.

When you develop a secure relationship with yourself—when you trust your perceptions, honour your needs, and maintain your boundaries—you naturally become less attracted to people who can't offer the same respect you give yourself.

This is why self-work isn't separate from changing your attraction patterns—it's the foundation. As you heal your relationship with yourself, your chemistry addiction naturally begins to lose its grip.

Bottom Line: New Chemistry is Possible

Yes, you can change what you're attracted to. Many people have successfully rewired their attraction patterns and found themselves genuinely drawn to partners who offer stability rather than chaos, consistency rather than intensity, and respect rather than drama.

The most beautiful part? When you've done this work, you discover that healthy relationships offer the most profound form of passion—one built on emotional safety rather than fear, genuine intimacy rather than intensity, and shared growth rather than power struggles.

That feeling might not match the familiar adrenaline rush of your old chemistry addiction, but it offers something far better: a connection that energizes rather than depletes you, deepens rather than deteriorates, and evolves rather than implodes.

Your future self is cheering you on from a peaceful, loving relationship where "drama" is something you watch on Netflix, not something you live through on a Tuesday night.

Research Spotlight: Studies on Relationship Satisfaction vs. Initial Attraction

If you're worried that giving up your addiction to intense chemistry means settling for a bland relationship, science has some reassuring news for you. Researchers have been studying the relationship between initial attraction and long-term satisfaction for decades, and their findings consistently reveal something that might surprise you: the qualities that create that initial spark are often entirely different from— and sometimes directly opposed to —the qualities that lead to lasting happiness.

Let's examine what the research reveals about the disconnect between what draws us in and what keeps us fulfilled.

The Passion Paradox: Early Intensity vs. Long-Term Satisfaction

In a landmark longitudinal study by Dr. Ted Huston at the University of Texas (the PAIR Project - Processes of Adaptation in Intimate Relationships), researchers followed couples from their wedding day through their first 13 years of marriage. One of the most striking findings? Couples who reported the most intense romantic feelings and passion initially were more likely to have divorced after 13 years.

That's right—the couples who were most "madly in love" early on were more likely to end up separated than those who reported more moderate, steady feelings.

Why? The researchers found that relationships built on high levels of romantic intensity often experienced sharper declines in satisfaction when that intensity naturally decreased. Essentially, these couples had nowhere to go but down from their honeymoon phase high. Meanwhile, couples with more moderate initial passion often experienced increasing satisfaction as their relationships deepened over time.

This doesn't mean passion is terrible—it just means that white-hot intensity isn't the reliable predictor of future happiness we often assume it to be.

The Attraction-Satisfaction Gap

Dr. Eli Finkel at Northwestern University coined the term "the attraction-satisfaction gap" after reviewing decades of relationship research. His team found that the traits people list as desirable in potential partners when they're in the attraction phase (physical appearance, social status, charisma) have surprisingly little overlap with the traits that predict relationship satisfaction when studied long-term (emotional stability, kindness, compatibility in values).

Practical Tool: The Attraction Reset Protocol

If you've realised your attraction compass needs recalibration, you're probably wondering: "Okay, but HOW exactly do I change what I'm attracted to?" It's one thing to understand theoretically that your chemistry addiction is leading you astray—it's another actually to rewire those deeply ingrained patterns.

That's where the Attraction Reset Protocol comes in. This isn't a vague suggestion to "just pick better partners." It's a concrete, step-by-step system that has helped thousands of my clients transform their attraction patterns from self-sabotage to self-enhancement.

The protocol consists of four phases, each with specific exercises and techniques. Think of it like physical therapy for your attraction patterns. If you follow the protocol consistently, you will experience change, even if the exercises sometimes feel uncomfortable or strange at first.

Let's dive in.

PHASE 1: PATTERN MAPPING (Duration: 1-2 Weeks)

Before changing your attraction patterns, you need a crystal-clear awareness of what they are. Most people have only a vague sense of their patterns ("I always pick jerks") without understanding the specific triggers, dynamics, and rewards that maintain these patterns.

Exercise 1: The Relationship Inventory

Create a detailed inventory of your last 3-5 significant attractions or relationships by answering these questions for each:

1. What initially attracted you to this person? Be specific about traits, behaviours, and the feelings they evoked.

2. When did you feel the most substantial chemistry? What was happening at those moments?

3. What relationship dynamic eventually emerged? (e.g., pursuer/distancer, caretaker/cared-for)

4. How did the relationship typically make you feel? (anxious, secure, excited, drained)

5. What needs were you hoping this person would meet?

6. What was the pattern of conflict or disconnection?

7. How did it end, or why is it problematic if ongoing?

PHASE 2: REWIRING TRIGGERS (Duration: 2-4 Weeks)

Now that you've mapped your patterns, it's time to begin actively rewiring your attraction triggers. This phase focuses on breaking the automatic associations between unhealthy traits and feelings of excitement or chemistry.

Exercise 1: The Red Flag Reframe

1. From your Relationship Inventory, identify the top 3-5 "red flag" traits that have consistently drawn you in but led to unhealthy relationships.

2. For each red flag, write down:

    - How this trait initially presents as positive or exciting

    - The eventual negative impact on your wellbeing

    - The more profound need you were hoping this trait would fulfil

    - A healthier trait that could meet that need

Exercise 2: Attraction Journaling Each time you feel a strong attraction or chemistry with someone new:

1. Note the specific behaviours or qualities triggering the attraction

2. Rate the intensity of the feeling (1-10)

3. Identify if any of your pattern "red flags" are present

4. Consciously remind yourself of the likely outcome based on your pattern mapping

5. Ask: "Is this familiar chemistry or healthy attraction?"

Exercise 3: Exposure Training This exercise helps retrain your nervous system to recognise healthy traits as attractive:

1. Create a list of traits that indicate relationship health (emotional availability, consistency, respect for boundaries, etc.)

2. Actively seek out examples of these traits in action (in friends' relationships, movies, books)

3. When you observe these traits, pause and consciously associate them with safety, attraction, and desirability

4. Practice visualising yourself feeling chemistry with someone displaying these healthy traits

PHASE 3: RECALIBRATING STANDARDS (Duration: 2-4 Weeks)

This phase focuses on establishing new criteria for what you allow into your emotional space. You're essentially creating a new operating system for your heart.

Exercise 1: The Partner Prototype Redesign

1. Create two detailed profiles:

    - Your "Default Attraction" prototype (the type you've historically been drawn to)

    - Your "Healthy Attraction" prototype (the type that would genuinely meet your needs)

2. For each prototype, describe:

    - How they handle conflict
    - How they express care
    - How they respond to your vulnerability
    - What daily life would feel like with them
    - The overall trajectory of a relationship with them

Exercise 2: The Trial Period Policy Implement a new standard for dating:

1. Establish a 30-day "evaluation period" for any new romantic interest

2. During this time, commit to:

    - Not becoming physically intimate
    - Observing them in different contexts and situations
    - Noting how they respond to minor challenges or disappointments
    - Checking in with trusted friends about your perceptions

3. After 30 days, formally assess: Does this person align more with your Default or Healthy prototype?

Exercise 3: Value-Based Screening

1. Identify your 5 core relationship values (e.g., honesty, mutual support, emotional openness)

2. Create specific, observable criteria for each value

3. Practice articulating these values in conversation

4. Develop 2-3 questions that help reveal alignment with each value

PHASE 4: SUSTAINABLE INTEGRATION (Duration: Ongoing)

The final phase is about integrating your new attraction patterns into your life for the long term, which requires internal and external support systems.

Exercise 1: The Attraction Support Team

1. Identify 2-3 people who:
    - Know your patterns well
    - Will be honest with you
    - Have healthy relationships themselves

2. Share your pattern mapping and new standards with them

3. Create a specific "check-in" protocol for when you're in the early stages with someone new

4. permit them to raise concerns if they notice your old patterns emerging

Exercise 2: The Feeling Dictionary Create a personal reference guide to distinguish between:

1. Chemistry vs. Compatibility

2. Intensity vs. Intimacy

3. Excitement vs. Security

4. Challenge vs. Growth

5. Passion vs. Sustainability

For each pair, define:

- How each one feels in your body

- What thoughts accompany each feeling

- The typical trajectory of relationships based on each

Exercise 3: Regular Pattern Audits Schedule a monthly "pattern audit" where you:

1. Review your current attractions and relationships

2. Assess alignment with your new standards

3. Celebrate progress and adjust as needed

4. Recommit to your healthy attraction goals

The most important thing to remember is that changing attraction patterns takes time. You're essentially rewiring neural pathways that have been reinforced for years. Be patient with yourself, celebrate small shifts in awareness, and trust that what feels forced at first will eventually become your new regular with consistent practice.

Your attraction patterns can change. Thousands have done this work successfully, and you can too. The relationship you deserve is waiting on the other side of this process.

CHAPTER 3:

Your Dating Blind Spots

What You Can't See Might Be Hurting You

We all have them—those relationship patterns so deeply ingrained that they're practically invisible to us. Like that lipstick on your teeth that everyone sees but no one mentions, dating blind spots can sabotage your love life while you remain blissfully (or miserably) unaware.

Think of dating blind spots as your personal relationship gremlins operating behind the scenes. At the same time, you wonder why you keep ending up binge-watching true crime documentaries alone on Friday nights, asking your cat, "Is it me?" (Spoiler alert: it's partly you, your blind spots, and your cat is judging you).

The Science of Selective Vision

Your blind spots aren't random—your brain carefully crafts them based on your early experiences, attachment style, and the narratives you've built about yourself and your relationships. Your brain is essentially a prediction machine, constantly scanning for evidence that confirms what you already believe while filtering out contradictory information.

This is why two people can experience the same relationship in completely different ways. One person might see "passionate debates" while the other experiences "constant fighting." One might notice an "independent spirit" while the other feels "emotional unavailability." We're all wearing relationship goggles calibrated by our unique psychological history.

Common Dating Blind Spots (And Yes, You Probably Have At least One)

1. The "I Can Fix Them" Blindness

The Blind Spot: You're magnetically drawn to people with "potential"—those who would be perfect if they just got therapy, quit drinking, resolved their commitment issues, or finished the novel they've been working on for seven years.

The Reality Check: You've cast yourself as the relationship renovation expert, but here's the uncomfortable truth: People change when THEY want to change. Your love, support, and strategically placed self-help books aren't magical transformation catalysts.

Secret Payoff: Focusing on fixing others keeps you safely distracted from your growth edges. Plus, when someone has "potential," you get to feel needed without the vulnerability of being fully seen.

Warning Signs You Have This Blind Spot:

- Your dating history reads like a rehabilitation centre intake log

- Friends introduce you to stable people, and you find them "boring."

- You regularly say, "You don't understand; they're different with me."

- Your therapist sighs heavily whenever you mention a new relationship

The Breakthrough Question: "If this person never changed a single thing, would I still choose them exactly as they are right now?"

2. The "Emotional Unavailability Detector"

The Blind Spot: You consistently find yourself attracted to emotionally unavailable people; whether they're still hung up on an ex, pathologically independent, or so career-focused, they schedule bathroom breaks in their Google calendar.

The Reality Check: Your attraction system is calibrated to recognise emotional distance as familiar and therefore "right," especially if your early attachment figures were inconsistently available. You've mistaken the anxiety of pursuit for the flutter of attraction.

Secret Payoff: When someone is emotionally unavailable, you get to experience the illusion of intimacy without the vulnerability of genuine intimacy. If they never fully show up, you never have to show up either fully.

Warning Signs You Have This Blind Spot:

- You're fluent in text analysis, frequently parsing messages for hidden meanings

- The phrase "I'm just really busy with work right now" makes you try harder

- You find yourself saying, "Things were amazing in the beginning" a lot

- You have lengthy relationships that never seem to progress beyond a certain point

The Breakthrough Question: "Do I spend more time thinking about this relationship than actually being in it?"

3. The "Chemistry Is King" Conviction

The Blind Spot: You believe real love begins with fireworks, butterflies, and that intoxicating feeling that makes you unable to eat or sleep. Without that initial explosion, you don't see the point in exploring a connection.

The Reality Check: What you're calling "chemistry" might be anxiety, familiarity with dysfunction, or your attachment system activating. The butterflies you chase might be warning flutters, not love signals.

Secret Payoff: Intense chemistry provides a neurochemical high that can become addictive. Plus, when relationships based solely on chemistry inevitably flame out, you get to remain safely convinced that passionate love doesn't last.

Warning Signs You Have This Blind Spot:

- You've dismissed potentially great partners within the first 30 minutes

- Your relationships are intense but short-lived

- You've used the phrase "when you know, you know" to justify questionable choices

- Your concept of passion necessarily includes some form of suffering

The Breakthrough Question: "What if sustainable love feels different from what I've been pursuing?"

4. The "My List Is Non-Negotiable" Lockdown

The Blind Spot: You have a detailed checklist of qualities your ideal partner must possess, from height requirements to career specifications to whether they enjoy both Thai food and camping. You rigidly evaluate potential matches against this list.

The Reality Check: While value alignment is important, your checklist might be filtering out compatible partners based on superficial criteria while failing to screen for genuinely essential qualities, such as emotional intelligence, conflict resolution skills, and capacity for growth.

Secret Payoff: Having an extensive list gives you the illusion of control and keeps you safely single while appearing to be actively searching.

Warning Signs You Have This Blind Spot:

- You've rejected someone for trivial reasons while ignoring major green flags
- Your list has gotten longer with each disappointing relationship
- You can immediately identify what's wrong with someone but struggle to articulate what you need
- You've been looking for the same specific type for years with no success

The Breakthrough Question: "Am I looking for a partner or a product I can order to specification?"

5. The "I'm Just Being Honest" Illusion

The Blind Spot: You pride yourself on "telling it like it is" and being "authentic," which often translates to blurting out unfiltered thoughts, oversharing inappropriately early, or being needlessly blunt under the guise of honesty.

The Reality Check: What you're calling honesty might be impulsivity, lack of boundaries, or using "truth" as a weapon. Genuine intimacy develops through gradual, appropriate disclosure, not emotional dumping.

Secret Payoff: When people react negatively to your honesty, you get to label them as unable to handle your authentic self, rather than examining how you're communicating.

Warning Signs You Have This Blind Spot:

- First dates often look like therapy sessions where you're both client and therapist
- You've said, "I'm just being honest", after saying something hurtful
- People seem overwhelmed by your communication style
- You believe vulnerability means revealing everything immediately

The Breakthrough Question: Is My 'Honesty' Building a Connection or Creating Distance?

6. The "All My Exes Are Psychos" Amnesia

The Blind Spot: You're convinced you've just had terrible luck in the partner department. Somehow, you've managed to date a statistically impossible string of toxic, crazy, or awful people, and you were the perfectly reasonable victim in each scenario.

The Reality Check: The common denominator in all your relationships is you. While you may have dated some genuinely difficult people, consistently attracting or being attracted to problematic partners suggests that you've patterns worth examining.

Secret Payoff: Blaming others allows you to avoid the uncomfortable work of self-reflection and change.

Warning Signs You Have This Blind Spot:

- You can't name your contribution to any past relationship breakdown
- Your breakup stories cast you as the flawless hero
- Friends seem hesitant when you describe your relationship history
- You keep having the "Why does this always happen to me?" conversation

The Breakthrough Question: "What's my role in choosing and maintaining these dynamics?"

7. The "Relationship Milestone Obsession"

The Blind Spot: You're so focused on reaching conventional relationship milestones (exclusivity by month three, meeting family by month six, engagement by year two) that you're not evaluating whether the relationship itself is healthy or fulfilling.

The Reality Check: You may be more invested in the relationship progression than in your actual partner. External validations, such as Instagram-worthy dates and "official" status updates, don't foster genuine intimacy.

Secret Payoff: Focusing on milestones gives you a sense of control and allows you to measure "success" without facing the messier, more nuanced work of building authentic connections.

Warning Signs You Have This Blind Spot:

- You've stayed in mediocre relationships because you'd invested a certain amount of time

- You feel anxiety if your relationship isn't "keeping pace" with others

- You've pushed for the next steps even when things didn't feel right

- You care more about how your relationship looks than how it feels

The Breakthrough Question: "If there were no external timeline or social validation, would I still want this relationship exactly as it is?"

8. The "I Don't Need Anyone" Independence

The Blind Spot: You pride yourself on being self-sufficient and independent, possibly building a life so complete that there's barely room for a partner. You may unconsciously sabotage relationships when they start to require vulnerability.

The Reality Check: What you're calling independence might be fear of dependence. Healthy relationships require interdependence—the ability to maintain selfhood while also being emotionally available and occasionally reliant on another person.

Secret Payoff: Extreme self-sufficiency protects you from the risk of rejection, abandonment, or having to compromise.

Warning Signs You Have This Blind Spot:

- You feel uncomfortable when someone tries to help or support you
- You're proud that you "don't need anyone"
- You unconsciously test partners by pulling away
- Your life is so carefully structured that a partner would struggle to fit in

The Breakthrough Question: "Am I independent by choice or by defense?"

How to Illuminate Your Blind Spots

Ready to shine some light into these dark corners? Here's how to begin:

1. The Friendship Mirror Method

Your close friends have front-row seats to your relationship patterns. Create a safe space for honest feedback with questions like:

- "What patterns have you noticed in my relationships?"

- "Is there anything I consistently miss about the people I date?"

- "What do you think I need in a partner versus what I think I want?"

Prepare yourself to listen without defensiveness (perhaps with a glass of wine and a pre-commitment not to shoot the messenger).

2. The Ex-Factor Analysis

While not all exes will offer helpful insights (and some should remain firmly in the past), a considerate analysis of previous relationships can reveal patterns. Ask yourself:

- Were there red flags I ignored early on?

- What unspoken expectations did I bring into this relationship?

- What role did I play in the dynamic that developed?

- Was I authentically myself or playing a version of myself I thought they wanted?

This isn't about blame—it's about pattern recognition.

3. The Attraction Inventory

For two weeks, keep track of who catches your eye—not just people you actually date, but anyone you feel drawn to. Note:

- What specific qualities initially drew you in?

- What assumptions did you make about them based on limited information?

- What familiar dynamic might this person represent?

This helps you recognise your attraction triggers before you're emotionally invested.

4. The Opposite Day Experiment

Challenge yourself to consider people who represent the opposite of your typical "type." This doesn't mean dating someone you find unappealing but rather questioning your automatic dismissals:

- If you always date artistic types, chat with someone in a technical field

- If you're drawn to intense personalities, give the quiet, steady person a chance

- If you like "project" partners, talk to someone who has their life relatively together

You might discover attractions you didn't know were possible when you step outside your pattern.

5. The Pattern Interruption Protocol

Once you identify a blind spot, create a specific plan to interrupt your typical response:

- If you tend to overlook red flags, commit to discussing concerns with a friend before getting serious

- If you mistake anxiety for attraction, institute a "slow dating" rule for yourself

- If you over-function for under-functioning partners, practice asking for help in small ways

- If you flee when things get emotionally intimate, commit to staying with the discomfort for increasing periods

Breaking patterns requires conscious intention until new habits form.

The Ultimate Blind Spot: Thinking It's Just About Finding the "Right Person"

Perhaps the biggest dating blind spot is believing that your relationship difficulties would be solved by simply finding the mythical "right person." This perspective keeps you focused on selection rather than connection, on finding rather than becoming.

The truth is that satisfying relationships aren't just discovered—they're created and maintained through mutual growth, communication, and intention. Your blind spots don't disappear when you find a great partner; they manifest in new contexts.

The good news? Every blind spot you illuminate becomes a potential strength. That tendency to see potential in others can evolve into discernment about who is doing the work versus just talking about it. That independence can transform into healthy interdependence when consciously managed.

Understanding your blind spots doesn't mean you're broken—it means you're human, with patterns formed from a lifetime of experiences. Bringing awareness to these patterns is the first step toward more conscious relationship choices and, ultimately, connections that reflect who you indeed are, not just who you've been programmed to seek.

So, grab that flashlight and start exploring those shadowy corners. Your future relationship self will thank you—probably while cuddling with someone who would have completely flown under your old relationship radar.

Common Cognitive Biases in Partner Selection

Have you ever had a friend who could spot relationship red flags from outer space when they appeared in someone else's relationship but somehow missed identical flags when they showed up in their own? Or perhaps you've found yourself saying, "I can't believe I didn't see that coming!" after a relationship ended, even though, in retrospect, all the signs were there from the very beginning.

Welcome to the fascinating world of dating blind spots—the cognitive biases that operate like invisible software running in the background of your love life, quietly influencing your decisions while remaining just outside your awareness.

These blind spots aren't character flaws or signs of low intelligence. Some of the most thoughtful and insightful people I know have significant blind spots in their dating lives. This is because cognitive biases are hardwired features of human psychology that affect everyone, regardless of IQ, emotional intelligence, or relationship experience.

The good news? Once you understand these biases, you can develop strategies to work around them—like installing an update to your mental operating system. Let's explore the most common blind spots that might be sabotaging your dating life.

Confirmation Bias: Finding Evidence for What You Already Believe

Confirmation bias is our tendency to notice, seek out, and remember information that confirms our existing beliefs while overlooking or dismissing information that contradicts them.

In dating, this bias works like a selective Instagram filter for reality. If you believe someone is perfect for you, you'll unconsciously highlight every piece of evidence supporting that belief while minimising or rationalising away contradictory information.

The Role of Self-Sabotage in Dating

You're three dates in with someone who seems genuinely great. They're attentive, share your values, and there's a comfortable chemistry between you. Everything is going suspiciously well. Then, like clockwork, the little voice in your head starts up:

"They're probably talking to other people." "They're going to discover the real me soon." "This is too good to be true." "It's only a matter of time before they lose interest."

Before you know it, you've picked a fight over nothing, stopped responding to texts, or found a minor flaw to obsess over until it becomes relationship-ending. Congratulations! You've successfully sabotaged yet another promising connection.

If this sounds familiar, you're not alone. Self-sabotage in dating is the relationship equivalent of setting fire to your own house because you're worried it might burn down someday.

What Is Self-Sabotage, exactly?

Self-sabotage in dating refers to behaviours and thought patterns that undermine potentially healthy relationships despite your conscious desire for connection. It's the gap between what you say you want— a loving relationship —and what your actions create: perpetual singlehood or a series of failed relationships.

One of the particularly frustrating aspects of self-sabotage is that it's often unconscious. You don't wake up thinking, "How can I ruin my dating life today?" Instead, these behaviours feel like reasonable responses to perceived threats or simply "the way things are" for you.

The Greatest Hits of Dating Self-Sabotage

Let's explore the most common ways people sabotage their own dating lives:

1. The Pre-emptive Strike

This classic form of self-sabotage involves ending relationships before they can end with you. The moment things start getting serious, you spot an "insurmountable" problem and make a hasty exit.

Identifying Your Personal Dating Myths

We all carry stories in our heads about how dating and relationships work. Some of these stories serve us well. Others... not so much. These are what I call "dating myths"—the unexamined beliefs that shape your relationship choices without your conscious awareness.

Dating myths aren't universal. Your personal collection of myths is as unique as your fingerprint, crafted from a blend of family messages, cultural conditioning, past heartbreaks, and that one romantic comedy you watched during a formative breakup when you were nineteen. (No? Just me?)

These myths operate like invisible software running in the background of your love life—they filter how you interpret romantic situations, influence who you're drawn to, and ultimately determine what feels right or wrong in relationships.

The tricky part? Most of us don't even realise these myths exist. We mistake them for objective reality rather than recognising them as stories we've internalised. Let's change that.

Common Dating Myths That Might Be Limiting You

Before we delve into your myth collection, let's examine some of the most common dating myths I've encountered during my years of working with clients. As you read these, notice if any feel familiar—like old friends you didn't realise were still hanging around.

The "One Perfect Person" Myth

The Myth: There is one perfect soulmate for everyone. When you meet them, you'll "know." Finding lasting love is primarily about locating this needle in the haystack of humanity.

How It Limits You: This myth creates impossible standards that no actual human can meet. It also encourages a passive approach to relationship formation—waiting for a connection to develop rather than actively cultivating one. When inevitable imperfections appear, you question whether you've found "the one" rather than working through usual relationship challenges.

Signs You Believe It: You find yourself endlessly searching for someone better, even when dating wonderful people. Minor incompatibilities can feel like evidence that you haven't seen "the right one" yet. You believe great relationships shouldn't require significant effort or growth.

Exercise: The Relationship Reality Check

This exercise is designed to help you identify and challenge the relationship beliefs that might be operating beneath your conscious awareness. Think of it as a reality check for the stories you've been telling yourself about love, dating, and relationships.

Step 1: Identify Your Relationship Absolutes

We all have relationship' truths" that we consider inevitable. These often contain words like "always," "never," "everyone," or "no one." Let's bring them into the light.

Complete these sentences quickly, writing down the first things that come to mind:

1. Relationships always...

2. Relationships never...

3. Men/women always...

4. Men/women never...

5. Love always...

6. If someone loves you, they'll never...

7. All couples eventually...

8. No relationship can survive...

9. Dating is always...

10. I'll never find someone who...

Review what you've written. These statements represent some of your core relationship beliefs—the "truths" you've internalised about how love works.

Step 2: Trace the Origins

For each absolute belief you've identified, ask yourself:

- Where did I learn this? (Family? Friends? Media? Past experiences?)

- What specific experiences "proved" this belief to me?

- Was I in an emotional state when I formed this belief that might have distorted my perception?

For example, if you wrote, "Men always leave eventually," you might realise this belief formed when your father left your family, was reinforced by a painful breakup in college, and solidified when watching a friend go through a divorce. That's a powerful constellation of experiences—but is it truly universal?

Step 3: Find the Exceptions

Now for the reality check part. For each belief, challenge yourself to find exceptions—either in your own experience or in relationships you've observed:

- Do I know any examples that contradict this belief?

- Have I ever experienced moments that don't fit this pattern?

- Do I know people whose relationships directly disprove this "rule"?

Expert Interviews: Therapists on Breaking Cycles

To provide deeper insight into how we can break free from repetitive relationship patterns, I interviewed five therapists who specialise in helping clients transform their dating lives. Their perspectives offer a window into the professional approaches that have helped thousands break free from self-defeating cycles.

Dr Maya Richardson, Attachment-Focused Therapist

Specialises in: Adult attachment patterns and relationship dynamics

On identifying attachment-based cycles:

"Most people come to therapy saying, 'I keep dating the wrong people,' but what's happening is they're repeatedly attracted to partners who confirm their existing attachment expectations. If you grew up with inconsistent caregiving, you may unconsciously seek partners who are hot and cold, as this dynamic feels familiar and activates your attachment system in a way that resonates.

The first step is helping clients recognize their attachment style and how it influences their partner selection. I often ask: 'How did you know you were loved as a child? What did you have to do to maintain a connection with important caregivers?' The answers frequently map directly onto their adult relationship patterns."

On rewiring attachment patterns:

"Breaking attachment-based cycles requires what we call 'earned secure attachment'—essentially rewiring your relationship blueprint through new experiences. This happens in two key environments: the therapeutic relationship and carefully chosen new relationships.

In therapy, clients experience consistent atonement and repair that may have been missing in formative relationships. This creates a template for what a healthy connection feels like. Meanwhile, I encourage them to practice 'dating against type'—consciously choosing partners.

Research Spotlight: Cognitive Behavioural Approaches to Dating

The field of Cognitive Behavioural Therapy (CBT) has revolutionised psychological treatment for various mental health issues over the past few decades. More recently, researchers and clinicians have applied these evidence-based principles to dating challenges and relationship patterns. Let's explore what the research tells us about cognitive behavioural approaches to transforming dating experiences.

The Cognitive Foundation of Dating Behaviours

At the heart of cognitive behavioural approaches is a simple yet powerful premise: our thoughts influence our emotions, which in turn drive our behaviours. In the context of dating, this creates a cycle that can either support healthy relationships or maintain dysfunctional patterns.

Research by Dr Jeffrey Young and colleagues on Early Maladaptive Schemas has identified how core beliefs formed early in life—such as "I'm unlovable" or "People will inevitably abandon me"—create cognitive filters that dramatically affect how we interpret dating interactions.

In a groundbreaking study published in the *Journal of Social and Personal Relationships*, researchers Knee, Patrick, and Lonsbary (2003) identified two fundamental relationship mindsets that influence dating behaviour:

1. **Destiny beliefs**: The view that relationships are either "meant to be" or not

2. **Growth beliefs**: The perspective that relationships develop through effort and working through challenges

Their research found that individuals with strong destiny beliefs tended to:

- Make rapid, definitive judgments about relationship potential
- Disengage quickly when faced with conflicts or differences
- Experience more volatile relationship satisfaction based on recent interactions

In contrast, those with growth mindsets showed:

- Greater willingness to work through compatibility challenges
- More stable relationship satisfaction across time
- Higher rates of relationship longevity

These findings suggest that cognitive frameworks significantly influence not just how we feel about dating experiences but the actual outcomes we create.

CHAPTER 4:

The Detox Period

When Breaking Bad Patterns Feels Worse Before It Gets Better

One of the most challenging—and often overlooked—parts of changing your dating patterns is the detox period. If you've ever tried to break a pattern of dating emotionally unavailable people, chasing relationship drama, or falling for potential rather than reality, you're probably familiar with this uncomfortable phase.

Picture this: You've had your big epiphany. Maybe it came after another situation crashed and burned, your friends staged an intervention about your dating choices, or you spent another birthday wondering why you're still stuck in the same relationship loops. Whatever sparked it, you've decided: No more toxic relationships! No more chasing people who can't commit! No more mistaking anxiety for chemistry!

And then... You feel terrible. Welcome to the relationship detox period.

Just like giving up caffeine or sugar, giving up your habitual relationship patterns triggers a withdrawal response. Your brain, quite literally, has become accustomed to the neurochemical cocktail produced by your typical relationship dynamics. The uncertainty, the highs and lows, the chase—all of these create powerful chemical responses in your brain that can become genuinely addictive. When you suddenly remove that source of stimulation, your brain protests loudly.

During this detox period, you might find yourself plagued by insistent thoughts about your ex. Not just any ex—usually the most chaotic, intense one. The one who kept you on your toes. The one who never quite committed but gave you just enough hope to stay invested. Your brain will highlight all their best moments while conveniently filtering out the nights you spent crying, the plans they cancelled, or how your friends worried about you.

You may also notice a profound sense of boredom with healthier, more potential partners. That lovely person who texts back consistently and wants to make plans? Your detoxing brain might register them as "no chemistry" or "too boring" because they don't trigger your usual stress responses. This is normal, if frustrating.

Some people experience actual physical symptoms during relationship detox—trouble sleeping, changes in appetite, restlessness, or a general sense of anxiety. Your emotional regulation may also be affected, leaving you more irritable or prone to mood swings than usual. Again, this is your brain adjusting to a new neurochemical normal.

The most dangerous part of the detox period is how convincingly your brain will try to talk you into going back to old patterns. "Maybe I was too harsh on my ex," it whispers. "Maybe one text wouldn't hurt," it suggests. "Maybe I'm meant to be alone because I just don't feel excited about healthier people," it argues. These thoughts aren't reality—they're withdrawal symptoms.

So, how do you get through this challenging phase? First, recognise it for what it is: temporary. The intensity of detox symptoms typically peaks within the first few weeks and gradually diminishes over the course of 1-3 months. Understanding the process helps you resist abandoning your new standards when discomfort hits.

Having support is crucial during this time. Whether it's friends who understand what you're doing, a therapist who specialises in relationship patterns, or even an online community focused on healthier relationships—don't try to white-knuckle through detox alone. When you feel the impulse to contact your former partner late at night, it is advisable to seek someone to provide support and help you resist the urge.

Creating alternate sources of good feelings helps, too. Your brain is missing its usual dopamine hits, so find healthier ways to stimulate your reward system, such as exercise, time in nature, creative pursuits, meaningful social connections, or accomplishing small goals. These activities help your brain develop new pathways for experiencing pleasure and excitement.

Mindfulness practices can be beneficial during detox. When cravings or romanticised memories arise, observe them without judgment instead of trying to suppress them (which usually backfires). Notice the thought ("I miss how exciting things were with Jamie"), acknowledge the feeling and let it pass without acting on it.

Perhaps most importantly, be patient and compassionate with yourself. Changing deeply ingrained attraction patterns isn't easy—if it were, self-help books wouldn't be a multi-billion dollar industry. Backslides happen. The occasional weak moment doesn't erase your progress. The path toward healthier relationship patterns rarely moves in a straight line.

Remember that what you're feeling isn't a sign that you're making a mistake by pursuing healthier relationships. It's evidence that you're disrupting patterns that weren't serving you. The discomfort is a form of growth in real-time—your brain rewires to find new sources of connection and pleasure.

The good news? People successfully navigate the detox period every day. You strengthen new neural pathways each time you resist the pull of old patterns. Eventually, what once felt foreign begins to feel normal. The drama that once seemed exciting is starting to look exhausting. And the steady, genuine connection that once seemed boring reveals its deeper, more sustainable form of chemistry.

Your future self—the one in a relationship that brings peace rather than chaos, connection rather than anxiety—is cheering you on through this detox period. They know something you're still learning: what waits on the other side is worth every uncomfortable moment of the journey.

The Science of Habit Breaking

So, you've identified your relationship patterns, explored your attraction triggers, and recognised the cognitive biases influencing your dating decisions. You're probably thinking, "Great! Now I'll stop doing all those unhelpful things and make better choices!"

If only it were that simple.

Here's the reality check: Awareness alone rarely changes behaviour. If it did, every person who realises smoking is harmful would quit instantly, every dieter would maintain their ideal weight, and everyone who's ever identified their problematic relationship patterns would immediately stop repeating them.

Yet here we are, intelligent humans, repeatedly doing things we know aren't good for us. Why? Because learning and doing live in different neighbourhoods of your brain, and they don't always communicate well.

This is where the Dating Detox comes in—a deliberate period of romantic abstinence designed to break the neurobiological cycles that keep you trapped in unhealthy relationship patterns. Let's explore the science behind why this detox period is so crucial and how to make it effective.

Why Your Brain Is Addicted to Your Dating Patterns

Think of your dating patterns as neural superhighways in your brain. These aren't just psychological preferences—they're physical neural pathways that have been reinforced over time through repetition. Each time you've been attracted to the same type of unavailable person, pursued the same kind of drama-filled relationship or responded to relationship stress with the exact coping mechanisms, you've strengthened these neural connections.

Neuroscientists have a saying: "Neurons that fire together, wire together." This principle, known as Hebbian learning, explains why patterns become more entrenched the more frequently they are repeated. Your brain quite literally becomes structured around your habits—including your dating habits.

Creating Your Dating Sabbatical

So, you've decided to take the plunge—or rather, take a break from plunging into one disappointing dating situation after another. Congratulations! Your dating sabbatical might be your most loving commitment in years. Now, let's make sure you design it for success rather than setting yourself up for the relationship equivalent of a crash diet that ends in a midnight ice cream binge and regretful swiping.

Planning Your Personalized Detox Protocol

Remember, this isn't a one-size-fits-all prescription. Your dating sabbatical should be tailored to your specific patterns, triggers, and goals. Here's how to create a detox that will work for you:

Step 1: Define Your Specific Parameters

First, get crystal clear about what you're taking a break from. A dating detox means different things to different people, depending on their patterns. Consider which of these elements you need to include in your sabbatical:

Core Detox Elements (Recommended for Everyone):

- Dating apps and websites

- First dates and romantic pursuits

- "Checking in" texts with exes

- Social media stalking of potential interests

- Hookups and casual sexual relationships

Additional Elements (Based on Your Patterns):

- Romantic movies and books (if you tend to idealise romance)

- Conversations about dating (if they trigger obsessive thinking)

- Environments where you typically pursue partners (certain bars, events)

- Alcohol (if it tends to weaken your dating boundaries)

- Specific friends who encourage unhealthy dating behaviours

Elena, a client who was addicted to the validation from dating apps, initially baulked at deleting them: "Can't I just not open them?" After three failed attempts at partial detox, she finally deleted the apps entirely and blocked them using screen time controls. "The complete break was what I needed. The apps being removed eliminated the constant temptation to 'just check' notifications.

Step 2: Set Your Duration and Intention

Like any sabbatical, your dating detox needs both a defined timeframe and a clear purpose. Without these elements, it's too easy to drift back into old patterns at the first sign of loneliness or boredom.

Timeframe Options:

- Starter Detox: 30 days (suitable for first-timers or those highly resistant)

- Standard Detox: 90 days (generally needed for meaningful neural rewiring)

- Deep Detox: 6 months (for entrenched patterns or after significant heartbreak)

- Milestone Detox: Until a specific life event or personal accomplishment

Your detox intention should focus on what you're moving toward, not just what you're avoiding. Compare these intentions:

- Weak: "I'm taking a break from toxic relationships."

- Strong: I'm creating space to reconnect with my authentic desires and develop a deeper relationship with myself, so I can ultimately attract healthier connections.

Marcos, who had been in a series of emotionally unavailable relationships, initially planned a 30-day break. "By day 25, I realised I was just counting down to dating again without having done any real work. I extended to 90 days, and that's when the actual changes started happening."

Step 3: Prepare Your Environment

Environmental cues powerfully influence behaviour. Set yourself up for success by modifying your surroundings to support your detox goals.

Digital Cleanup:

- Delete dating apps (not just remove them from your home screen)

- Archive or delete text chains with exes or recent dates

- Mute or unfollow social media accounts that trigger romantic longing

- Set up screen time limits for social media browsing

- Clear your browser history and favourites related to dating sites

Physical Space Reset:

- Remove objects that trigger thoughts of past relationships (or box them up temporarily)

- Rearrange furniture to create new spatial patterns and associations

- Create dedicated spaces for the self-development activities you'll be prioritising

- Stock up on supplies for healthy coping mechanisms (books, art materials, exercise equipment)

Social Environment Management:

- Inform supportive friends about your detox and ask for their accountability

- Temporarily distance yourself from friends who undermine your goals

- Find or create social activities that don't revolve around dating or "finding someone."

Sydney, who kept breaking her detox when hanging out with certain friends, created a "dating detox social calendar" with alternative plans. "I knew Friday nights with my single friends would be my weak point, so I signed up for a pottery class that met Friday evenings instead. Having the prepaid commitment helped me follow through."

Step 4: Design Your Replacement Activities

Nature abhors a vacuum. If you remove dating without adding meaningful alternatives, your brain will revolt against the perceived deprivation. Your replacement activities should serve two purposes:

1. Provide healthy sources of the same rewards you seek from dating (connection, excitement, validation)

2. Support personal growth in areas that will ultimately lead to healthier relationships

For Connection:

- Deepen existing friendships through consistent, meaningful interaction

- Join interest-based communities (book clubs, hiking groups, volunteer organisations)

- Reconnect with family members in new, adult ways

- Consider therapy or support groups focused on relationship patterns

For Excitement/Stimulation:

- Try physically challenging activities (rock climbing, dance classes, martial arts)

- Pursue creative expression (writing, music, art, photography)

- Plan adventures or exploration (even in your city)

- Learn challenging new skills that create flow states

For Validation/Self-Worth:

- Set and achieve progressive goals in areas of personal interest

- Engage in activities where you can help others

- Create measurable metrics for tracking personal growth

- Practice self-acknowledgment and celebration of small wins

Jamie, who realised she dated for external validation, began taking singing lessons during her detox. "Performing at my first recital gave me the same rush I used to get from someone new finding me attractive, but this time, the high came from my accomplishment."

Step 5: Establish Your Support System

Even with the best intentions and preparation, you'll face moments when your resolve weakens. Having specific support mechanisms in place makes the difference between a temporary craving and a complete detox collapse.

Your Detox Support Team:

- Designate 2-3 specific friends you can text or call when urges strike

- Consider working with a therapist who specialises in attachment or relationship patterns

- Join online communities focused on dating detoxes or relationship healing

- Find an accountability partner who's also taking a dating break

- Create check-in mechanisms (weekly journaling, monthly review with a friend)

Emergency Protocols:

- Create a specific list of steps to take when feeling desperate to break your detox

- Write a letter to your future self explaining why you started this detox

- Develop an "urge surfing" meditation or breathing practice

- Have pre-planned distractions for high-risk times (Friday nights, after drinking)

Alex, who kept breaking no-contact with an ex, finally found success with a buddy system. "I gave a friend $200 and told them if I contacted my ex, they would donate it to a political cause I despised. Having something concrete on the line made me pause long enough for the urge to pass."

Step 6: Track Your Progress and Insights

Without reflection, a dating detox can become merely a period of abstaining from dating rather than a transformative experience. Create systems to track both your adherence and your evolving awareness.

Tracking Methods:

- Daily journaling with specific prompts about patterns and triggers

- Weekly reflection on what you're learning about yourself

- Monthly review of how your relationship with yourself is changing

- Voice memos capturing insights as they arise

- Visual tracking of detox streaks and milestones

Questions to Regularly Explore:

- What am I learning about the difference between my relationship needs and wants?

- How is my definition of attraction evolving?

- What patterns am I noticing when I feel the urge to date or connect?

- What new aspects of myself am I discovering or developing?

- How are my feelings about past relationships changing?

Jordan, initially sceptical about journaling, created a voice memo system instead. "Every night before bed, I'd record a 2-minute reflection on my day. After three months, I listened to them in order and was shocked at how my perspective had evolved."

Step 7: Plan Your Reintegration Strategy

The end of your formal detox isn't the end of your journey—it's a transition to more conscious relationship choices. Without a clear reintegration plan, it's easy to slide right back into old patterns.

Before Ending Your Detox, Define:

- Specific green and red flags based on what you've learned

- New dating boundaries you'll implement

- How you'll pace new relationships (communication frequency, physical intimacy timeline)

- Deal-breakers you now recognise

- Signs that would indicate you need another detox period

Gradual Reintegration Strategies:

- Start with limited, structured dating (one app, specific days for checking)

- Create a "dating budget" (time, money, emotional energy you'll invest)

- Establish regular check-ins with yourself or an accountability partner

- Plan continued self-development alongside dating

Maya, after six months of detox, created a detailed re-entry plan. I decided to use only one dating app, check it only on Tuesdays and Thursdays, and limit myself to one date per week. This structure helped me stay conscious about dating rather than falling into the old addiction."

The Reality Check: Expect Challenges

Even the most carefully planned detox will include moments of doubt, loneliness, and temptation. These aren't signs of failure—they're expected parts of the process.

Common challenges include:

- The "everyone else is pairing up" panic (especially around holidays)
- The "am I wasting my prime years" anxiety
- The "maybe I'm meant to be alone" spiral
- The "one little exception won't hurt" rationalisation
- The "I've changed enough already" impatience

These moments require self-compassion rather than rigid perfectionism. If you slip up, analyse what triggered the lapse, adjust your protocol accordingly, and continue your detox without shame spirals.

Remember: The goal isn't perfect adherence to arbitrary rules. The goal is to create enough space from unhealthy patterns so that you can consciously choose a new path in your relationships. Whether that takes exactly 90 days or includes a few detours along the way, the journey itself is reshaping your future relationships in profound ways.

Your future self—the one in a relationship that energises rather than depletes you—will thank you for this investment in becoming the partner you want to attract.

Creating New Neural Pathways

Picture your brain as a dense forest. Over the years, you've walked the same relationship path so many times that it has become a well-worn trail—easy to find and follow without much thought. Meanwhile, paths with healthier potential remain overgrown and difficult to navigate. Your dating detox isn't just about avoiding the familiar trail but actively creating new paths through the wilderness.

Neuroplasticity in action is your brain's remarkable ability to reorganise itself by forming new neural connections. Let's explore how to leverage this capacity to rewire your relationship brain during your dating sabbatical.

The Neuroscience of Building New Pathways

Contrary to long-held beliefs that adult brains are fixed and unchangeable, modern neuroscience has definitively shown that our brains remain plastic, or changeable, throughout our lives. Dr. Norman Doidge, author of The Brain That Changes Itself, describes neuroplasticity as "one of the most extraordinary discoveries of the twentieth century."

Here's how it works in the context of your relationship patterns:

1. **Neural pruning:** When you stop using specific neural pathways (such as your habitual dating patterns), those connections begin to weaken—a process known as "neural pruning."

2. **Hebbian learning:** When you repeatedly practice new thought patterns and behaviours, you strengthen the neural connections associated with them. As neuroscientist Donald Hebb famously said, "Neurons that fire together wire together."

3. **Competitive plasticity:** Your brain has limited real estate. When you build new neural pathways, they

compete with old ones for space and resources. The paths you use most frequently win this competition.

This science explains why simply gaining insight into your patterns isn't enough—you need to actively build alternative neural pathways through consistent, repetitive practice of new ways of thinking and behaving.

The Building Blocks of New Neural Pathways

Creating new relationship-related neural pathways involves four key elements:

1. Conscious Attention

Neuroplasticity begins with focused attention. Your brain prioritises building neural pathways for things you pay deliberate attention to.

Practice: The Relationship Lens Shift

Set a daily reminder to spend 5 minutes deliberately noticing:

- Healthy relationship dynamics around you (between friends, family, strangers, and even TV characters)

- Qualities in others that support emotional safety rather than drama

- Your responses to various relationship scenarios

I'll organise this with an introduction that explains the importance of journaling during the detox phase, followed by several categories of journaling prompts targeting different aspects of the detox experience. Each category will feature multiple specific prompts that are thought-provoking and designed to facilitate self-discovery and transformation.

The tone should be friendly, encouraging, and insightful - matching the voice established in previous sections of the book. I'll include some examples of how these prompts might help readers based on the "case study" approach used elsewhere in the book.

Journaling Prompts for the Detox Phase

Journaling isn't just a way to fill the time you're no longer spending swiping and dating—it's a powerful tool for rewiring your relationship with yourself and others. Research by Dr. James Pennebaker at the University of Texas has consistently demonstrated that expressive writing can help individuals process emotions, gain insights, and even improve their physical health.

During your dating detox, journaling serves multiple crucial functions:

- It creates a record of your transformation journey

- It provides an outlet for processing emotions that arise

- It helps identify patterns you might otherwise miss

- It makes unconscious thoughts and beliefs conscious

- It reinforces new neural pathways through written repetition

The key to effective journaling isn't writing perfect prose or even writing every day—it's asking yourself questions that bypass your usual thinking patterns and access deeper insights. Think of these prompts as doorways into rooms in your mind you rarely visit.

I've organized these prompts into categories that correspond with different aspects of your detox journey. Don't feel obligated to answer all of them—choose the ones that create that feeling of "Hmm, I've never quite thought about it that way" when you read them.

Week One: Pattern Recognition Prompts

These initial prompts help you clearly identify the patterns you're working to change:

1. **Without judging yourself, describe the most consistent relationship pattern that has appeared in your dating life. When did you first notice it?**

2. **Think of your three most significant relationships or dating experiences. What similarities do you notice in how they began, progressed, and ended?**

3. **If your dating history were a movie, what would be the recurring theme? Who would you cast as yourself, and what role would you like to play?**

4. **Imagine your future self has successfully broken your current relationship patterns. What would they want to tell you about what you're not seeing right now?**

5. What are the consistent complaints you have about dating, and what might this reveal about your patterns?

Week Two: Origins & Influences Prompts

These prompts help you explore where your relationship patterns originated:

1. What was your first understanding of what love looks like? Where did this image come from?

2. Describe your parents' or caregivers' relationship. What aspects of their dynamic do you see in your relationships?

3. What were you taught (directly or indirectly) about your worth in relationships? Who or what taught you this?

4. What did you learn about boundaries from your family of origin? How has this affected your dating life?

5. When you feel triggered or emotionally activated in dating scenarios, what childhood feelings do this most remind you of?

Week Three: Needs & Desires Prompts

These prompts help clarify what you truly want, separate from habitual patterns:

1. If you were to remove all external pressures and expectations, what would your ideal relationship look like?

2. What needs have you been trying to meet through dating that you could begin to meet on your own?

3. What aspects of yourself do you hide when dating? What would it feel like to be fully seen and accepted?

4. When do you feel most content and at peace when alone? How might this inform what you truly value?

5. What are you afraid might happen if you stopped pursuing relationships altogether? What does this fear tell you?

Week Four: Attachment & Triggers Prompts

These prompts explore your attachment style and emotional reactions:

1. When you feel insecure in a relationship, what explicitly triggers this feeling? What early experiences might this connect to?

2. How do you typically respond when you feel abandoned or rejected? What would a healthier response look like?

3. In what ways do you abandon yourself when in a relationship? What parts of yourself do you tend to neglect?

4. When do you feel most anxious or avoidant in relationships? What beliefs are activated in these moments?

5. What would it mean to be securely attached to yourself first before seeking attachment to another person?

Week Five: Values & Boundaries Prompts

These prompts help establish more precise values and healthier boundaries:

1. What values have you compromised in past relationships? How would honouring these values change your dating choices?

2. What boundaries do you struggle to maintain? What fears arise when you envision enforcing them consistently?

3. What are your non-negotiables in a relationship? Which of these have you previously treated as negotiable?

4. What do you need to feel safe and respected in a relationship? How can you communicate these needs more effectively?

5. What personal practices or rituals would help you maintain your sense of self when you start dating again?

Week Six: Integration & Moving Forward Prompts

These prompts help consolidate insights and prepare for mindful re-entry to dating:

1. What are the three most important insights you've gained during this detox period? How will they change your approach to relationships?

2. How will you recognise old patterns if they begin to emerge again? What specific signs will you watch for?

3. What specifically do you want to do differently when you start dating again? What concrete actions will support this?

4. What qualities in yourself have you developed or discovered during this detox that you want to maintain?

5. Write a letter to your future dating self with compassionate guidance about maintaining your growth and honouring your authentic needs.

These prompts are designed to build upon one another, helping you progress from recognition to understanding to integration. Remember that the most valuable insights often come from the prompts that feel slightly uncomfortable to answer—that's usually a sign you're touching on something important.

Research Spotlight: Studies on Habit Formation and Change

The success of your dating detox depends mainly on understanding how habits form and change. While we often think about dating patterns as preferences or choices, they're deeply ingrained habits operating at a neurological level. Let's explore what science reveals about how habits function and how they can be transformed.

formation **The Neuroscience of Habit Formation**

At the neural level, habits are physical structures in your brain. Research by Dr Ann Graybiel at MIT has mapped how habit circuits form in a region called the basal ganglia—an ancient brain structure involved in the movement, reward, and automatic behaviours. Using advanced imaging techniques, her team literally watched habits form as neural pathways strengthened with repetition.

What's fascinating about Graybiel's research is the discovery that once a habit circuit is established, it's never entirely erased. This explains why old dating patterns can feel so persistent—the neural pathways always remain, even when dormant. The good news? Her research also shows that new habit circuits can be built that effectively override the old ones when given enough reinforcement.

A groundbreaking study by Dr. Kyle Smith and Dr. Graybiel, published in Neuron, demonstrated that habits are stored as complete chunks of automatic behaviour. This means your dating habits aren't just individual behaviors but entire behavioral sequences—from how you select potential partners to how you communicate to how you respond to relationship stress—all linked together in automated neural packages.

The Habit Loop: Trigger, Routine, Reward

Charles Duhigg popularised research on the "habit loop" from studies at MIT, which identified three critical components of any habit:

1. **The Trigger (or Cue):** The stimulus that initiates the habitual behaviour

2. **The Routine:** The behavior itself

3. **The Reward:** The benefit that reinforces the habit

In dating, these loops might look like:

- **Trigger:** Feeling lonely on Friday night

- **Routine:** Redownloading dating apps and swiping for hours

- **Reward:** Brief dopamine hits from matches and messages

Case Studies: Success Stories from the Detox Period

Theory is helpful, but sometimes what we need is proof that transformation is possible. The following case studies showcase real people (with names and identifying details changed) who completed their dating detoxes and experienced meaningful change. Their stories illustrate not just the challenges of the process but the remarkable shifts that can happen when you commit to breaking old patterns.

Maya: Breaking the Anxious Attachment Cycle

Background: Maya, 34, had a clear pattern of becoming intensely attached to emotionally unavailable men. Her relationships followed a predictable trajectory: initial mutual interest, growing anxiety as the man pulled away, escalating efforts to secure connection, and eventually, painful endings that reinforced her fear of abandonment. Despite therapy and self-help books, she couldn't break the pattern.

Detox Length: 90 days

Key Challenges:

- Intense loneliness during the first month

- Strong urge to reach out to her most recent ex

- Difficulty distinguishing between genuine connection and anxious attachment

- Fear that she was "missing opportunities" while on detox

Breakthrough Strategies:

1. **Body-based awareness practice:** Maya developed a daily check-in to identify her physical sensations of anxiety versus genuine attraction. She mapped how anxiety felt in her body (chest tightening, shallow breathing) versus authentic connection (relaxed shoulders, full breathing).

2. **Emotional regulation toolkit:** She created specific techniques for moments when attachment anxiety peaked, including a "nervous system reset" of cold water on her face followed by slow breathing.

3. **Systematic past review:** Using a structured format, she examined past relationships to identify exactly when anxiety began in each relationship and what specific partner behaviors triggered her attachment system.

4. **Self-attunement development:** Rather than seeking external validation, she practiced identifying and meeting her own emotional needs first.

Key Insights: During her third month of detox, Maya had a profound realization: "I discovered that what I called 'chemistry' was actually anxiety. The men I thought I was most attracted to were the ones who created the same emotional uncertainty I experienced with my father growing up. What felt like passion was fear of abandonment."

Jordan: Escaping the Perfection-Rejection Loop

Background: Jordan, 29, was caught in a cycle of brief, intense relationships that never lasted more than three months. He'd approach dating with impossibly high standards, finding initial "perfect matches" who inevitably revealed human flaws, triggering his disillusionment and withdrawal. Though successful professionally, he couldn't understand why his romantic life was filled with disappointment and disconnection.

Detox Length: 6 months

Key Challenges:

- Intense boredom and identity crisis when not actively dating

- Strong urge to download dating apps "just to check"

- Persistent belief that "the perfect person" was out there if only he searched harder

- Social pressure as friends paired off and questioned his single status

Breakthrough Strategies:

1. **Values clarification exercise:** Jordan systematically distinguished between his authentic relationship values and the superficial criteria he'd used to select partners.

2. **Idealization awareness practice:** He developed a technique to catch himself whenever he began mentally idealising potential partners, replacing this with conscious reality-checking.

3. **Gradual exposure to imperfection:** Through friendships, he practiced accepting others' flaws without judgment or withdrawal.

4. **Inner critic dialogue:** He identified the critical inner voice that constantly evaluated others and developed a compassionate counter-voice.

Key Insights: Four months into his detox, Jordan wrote: "I realized I wasn't actually afraid of choosing the wrong person—I was afraid of being disappointed, which felt inevitable. My perfectionism was a shield against vulnerability. What I called 'high standards' was actually fear of intimacy disguised as discernment."

Damon: Breaking the Emotional Unavailability Cycle

Background: Damon, 38, had mastered keeping partners at arm's length. Though charismatic and successful in the initial dating stages, he would become distant when relationships deepened, often working late, creating conflicts before important events, or mentally checking out. Despite genuinely wanting a connection, he sabotaged every relationship that threatened his emotional safety.

Detox Length: 1 year

Key Challenges:

- Extreme discomfort with solitude and self-reflection
- Strong impulse to date casually while claiming to be "working on himself"
- Physical anxiety symptoms when confronting deeper emotions
- Resistance to seeking professional help despite recognising the pattern

Breakthrough Strategies:

1. **Emotional vocabulary expansion:** He systematically worked to identify and name his emotions with greater precision beyond "fine," "stressed," or "annoyed."

2. **Graduated vulnerability practice:** He built emotional openness through structured sharing exercises, beginning with trusted friends before eventual dating.

3. **Pattern interruption techniques:** He developed specific strategies for moments when he felt the urge to distance, including direct communication scripts.

4. **Somatic release work:** Through body-based practices, he learned to identify and release tension that stored emotional avoidance.

Key Insights: Nine months into his detox, Damon wrote: "I realised my fear wasn't actually about getting hurt by others—it was about facing parts of myself I'd been running from for decades. What I called 'needing space' was actually panic about being truly seen. I wasn't protecting myself from others' rejection; I was rejecting myself first."

These individuals discovered that their dating patterns were deeply rooted in their neurobiology, past experiences, and unconscious belief systems. Their success came not just from avoiding dating but from using that space to develop new neural pathways, emotional responses, and self-awareness that fundamentally changed their approach to relationships.

CHAPTER 5:

Dating Yourself First

Self-Relationship as the Foundation

Remember how, in elementary school, teachers would say, "You have to love yourself before others can love you"? And remember how you probably rolled your eyes so hard they nearly fell out of your head? It turns out those well-meaning teachers were onto something—they just packaged it in a way guaranteed to make any self-respecting eight-year-old gag.

Now that we're adults with relationship battle scars and dating app fatigue, it's time to revisit this concept with fresh eyes. The truth is, your relationship with yourself isn't just a fluffy self-help concept—it's the actual blueprint for every other relationship in your life.

Consider this: You are the common denominator in all your relationships. The patterns you've identified in previous chapters. They don't just exist "out there" in the dating world. They're expressions of how you relate to yourself, projected onto the screen of romantic connection.

I can already hear some of you protesting: "But I'm great on my own! It's only in relationships that things get messy." I get it. You might be incredibly self-sufficient, triumphant in your career, surrounded by friends, and capable of assembling IKEA furniture without shedding a tear. But self-sufficiency isn't the same as having a healthy relationship with yourself.

Consider this: Would you date someone who speaks to you the way you talk to yourself? Would you stay with a partner who sets the expectations for you that you set for yourself? Would you feel loved by someone who offers you the same level of compassion, patience, and understanding that you provide to others?

For many of us, the honest answer is a resounding "hell no." We would dump that critical, demanding partner in a heartbeat—yet we stay in a lifelong relationship with ourselves where these dynamics are the daily norm.

This is why dating yourself first isn't just a cute way to fill time during your dating sabbatical—it's the essential work of creating a new template for a relationship, beginning with the most important one: the one with yourself.

Developing Self-Compassion and Worth

At the heart of any lasting relationship transformation is a fundamental shift in how you relate to yourself. Research consistently shows that the quality of our relationships with others reflects the quality of the relationship we have with ourselves. During your dating detox, developing genuine self-compassion and a solid sense of intrinsic worth becomes an essential foundation.

The Science of Self-Compassion

Dr. Kristin Neff, the pioneering researcher on self-compassion, distinguishes it from self-esteem in essential ways. While self-esteem is based on positive evaluation and achievement, self-compassion involves treating yourself with the same kindness and understanding you would offer a good friend during difficult times.

Her research demonstrates that self-compassion consists of three core components:

1. **Self-kindness vs. Self-judgment**: Offering warmth and understanding to yourself rather than harsh criticism

2. **Common humanity vs. Isolation**: Recognizing that suffering and personal failure are part of the shared human experience

3. **Mindfulness vs. Over-identification**: Maintaining a balanced awareness of painful thoughts without suppressing or exaggerating them

Studies show that people with higher self-compassion demonstrate:

- Greater emotional resilience

- Lower anxiety and depression

- More authentic relationship behaviours

- Less need for external validation

Breaking the Worthiness-Achievement Link

Many people caught in unhealthy dating patterns have unconsciously linked their worth to external factors, such as relationship status, partner quality, desirability, or romantic success. This creates a fragile foundation where self-worth fluctuates based on dating outcomes.

The key shift during detox involves separating your inherent worth from your relationship experiences. This means:

- Recognizing your value exists regardless of relationship status
- Identifying how you've measured your worth through others' responses
- Challenging beliefs that tie your worthiness to romantic success
- Developing internal sources of validation and meaning

Practical Self-Compassion Exercises

1. **The Self-Compassion Letter**: Write to yourself from the perspective of an unconditionally loving friend, offering understanding without judgment, about your dating struggles.

2. **Compassionate Touch**: Place your hand on your heart during moments of relationship pain or loneliness,

acknowledging your suffering with gentle physical touch.

3. **Worth Inventory**: List your qualities, contributions, and values that exist independently of anyone else's recognition or validation.

4. **Reframing Exercise**: Practice transforming self-critical thoughts ("I'm unlovable") into self-compassionate alternatives ("Many people struggle with finding partnership, and this difficulty doesn't diminish my worth").

5. **Morning Affirmation**: Begin each day with: "I am worthy of love exactly as I am. My worth is inherent and unconditional."

The paradox many discover during detox is that developing this internal relationship of compassion and worth creates the foundation for healthy partnerships. When you no longer need relationships to feel worthy, you're free to choose them from a place of wholeness rather than lack.

Designing a Life That Attracts the Right Partner

Let's address a common misconception: "working on yourself" during your dating sabbatical isn't about making yourself more attractive so the right person will choose you. It's about creating a life that:

1. You love regardless of relationship status

2. Naturally aligns with the kind of relationship you want

This shift in perspective changes everything. Instead of moulding yourself to appeal to some imagined future partner, you're building a life that reflects your authentic values and brings you genuine fulfilment. Paradoxically, this makes you far more likely to attract compatible partners.

The Magnetic Effect of an Authentic Life

Think of it this way: The life you create serves as a sorting mechanism for potential partners. When you live authentically, you naturally attract people who resonate with the real you, while repelling those who don't.

Daniel had spent years trying to be who he thought women wanted—downplaying his passion for science fiction, pretending to enjoy clubbing and presenting a more extroverted persona than felt natural. Not surprisingly, the relationships that resulted were uncomfortable and ultimately disappointing.

During his dating detox, Daniel reconnected with his authentic interests and preferences. He joined a sci-fi book club, started hiking on weekends instead of forcing himself to go to clubs, and embraced his more introverted nature.

"I worried I was making myself less dateable," he admitted. "But when I eventually started dating again, I was amazed by the difference. I met people in contexts where I was comfortable being myself, and they were attracted to the actual me, not some performance of who I thought I should be."

The Fulfilment Gap

Many people approach dating with a "fulfilment gap" they hope a relationship will fill. They put important aspects of their lives on hold, creating a void they expect a partner to address somehow:

- Once I'm in a relationship, I'll finally have someone to travel with.

- When I have a partner, I'll have someone to attend events with.

- "I'll explore that interest when I have someone to do it with."

This creates two problems:

1. It puts an impossible burden on future relationships to fulfil multiple suspended needs

2. It makes you more likely to choose someone—anyone—to fill the growing void

During your dating sabbatical, one of your most important tasks is identifying and addressing these fulfilment gaps.

The Full Life Inventory

Complete this exercise to identify areas where you might be waiting for a relationship to bring fulfilment:

1. List the experiences, activities, and forms of connection that are important to you

2. For each one, rate how actively it's present in your life now (1-10)

3. For items rated below 6, ask: "Am I waiting for a relationship to experience this?"

4. For each "yes," create a specific plan to bring this element into your life now

Tina realised she'd been postponing travel, putting off dinner parties, and even delaying redecorating her apartment because she was waiting to do these things "when" she was in a relationship. During her dating sabbatical, she took a solo trip to Portugal, hosted monthly potlucks for friends, and created a home that reflected her aesthetic rather than waiting for some future partner's input.

"By the time I started dating again, I didn't have this desperate energy of needing someone to complete my life," she explained. I was dating from a place of already being fulfilled, looking for someone to share my already good life with rather than someone to make it better.

The Partner Prototype vs. Relationship Vision Distinction

Another powerful shift occurs when you focus less on the characteristics of your ideal partner and more on the quality of the relationship you want to create.

Many people have detailed lists of qualities they seek in a partner but only vague notions about what daily life in the relationship would feel like. This keeps them focused on shopping for specific attributes rather than building capacity for certain kinds of connections.

Try this perspective shift:

Instead of asking: "What kind of person do I want to be with?" **Ask:** "What kind of relationship do I want to create?" **And then:** "What kind of person would be capable of and interested in creating that with me?" **Ultimately, how can I develop my capacity to create and sustain such a relationship?**

This approach fundamentally changes how you use your dating sabbatical. Instead of waiting to meet the right person, you're actively developing your ability to co-create the right relationship when you do meet someone compatible.

Malik had always focused on finding someone with the right looks, career, and interests. During his sabbatical, he shifted his focus to envisioning the relationship dynamics he wanted: mutual support for personal growth, comfortable silence alongside deep conversation, and a balance of independence and interdependence.

"I realised I needed to develop these capacities in myself first," he said. I couldn't expect to create a relationship with space for independence if I didn't know how to be happy and independent. I couldn't expect deep conversations if I wasn't willing to be vulnerable."

Exercise: The Ideal Relationship with Yourself

This exercise helps you create a concrete vision of the relationship you want to develop with yourself during your dating sabbatical. Just as you might envision qualities you want in a partner, this helps you define how you want to relate to yourself.

Step 1: The Relationship Assessment

First, evaluate your current relationship with yourself by rating the following aspects from 1-10:

- How well do you listen to your own needs?
- How kindly do you speak to yourself?
- How reliably do you keep commitments to yourself?
- How well do you acknowledge and process your emotions?
- How effectively do you advocate for your interests?
- How much do you appreciate your strengths and accomplishments?
- How compassionately do you respond to your mistakes and failures?
- How well do you respect your boundaries?

This assessment reveals both strengths to build upon and areas for growth to focus on during your sabbatical.

Step 2: The Ideal Dynamic Visualization

Imagine your relationship with yourself as a relationship between two people—the part of you that provides care and the part that receives it. In your journal, describe:

1. What would the ideal dynamic between these parts look like?

2. How would the caring part respond when you make mistakes?

3. What would this part do when you're facing fear or insecurity?

4. How would it react when you're tempted to return to old patterns?

5. What would it consistently help you remember about your worth?

Be as specific and detailed as possible, creating a clear vision of the self-relationship you want to develop.

Step 3: The Daily Practices Commitment

Based on your assessment and visualisation, identify 3-5 specific daily practices to strengthen your relationship with yourself. These might include:

- A morning check-in with yourself about how you're feeling and what you need

- A self-compassion break when you notice self-criticism

- A daily act of self-respect, such as keeping a promise to yourself or honouring a boundary.

- An evening appreciation practice, noting things you handled well that day

- A weekly "relationship date" with yourself for deeper reflection

The key is choosing practices that address your specific growth areas and feel genuinely supportive rather than like another set of "shoulds."

Step 4: The Relationship Agreement

Finally, create a formal agreement with yourself for this sabbatical period. Write it down in the form of commitments from you to you:

"I commit to speaking to myself with the same kindness I would offer a close friend." I commit to checking in with my emotional needs daily and responding to them with care and consideration. I commit to maintaining my boundaries, even when it's uncomfortable.

Sign and date this agreement as a symbol of your commitment to this most essential relationship.

Jenna found this exercise transformative: "Creating an actual relationship agreement with myself completely changed how I approached my sabbatical. Instead of just trying to avoid dating, I had a positive focus—building this primary relationship with myself. By the time I started dating again, the way I treated myself had become the template for how I expected to be treated by others."

Research Spotlight: Self-Determination Theory and Relationship Success

The importance of developing your relationship with yourself isn't just feel-good advice—it's supported by decades of research in motivation and psychological well-being, mainly through the framework of Self-Determination Theory (SDT).

Developed by psychologists Edward Deci and Richard Ryan, SDT identifies three universal psychological needs that are essential for well-being:

1. **Autonomy:** The sense that you're acting from choice and self-determination rather than external control

2. **Competence:** The experience of effectiveness in dealing with your environment

3. **Relatedness:** Feeling connected to and cared about by others

Research applying Self-Determination Theory (SDT) to relationships has yielded fascinating insights into why developing a relationship with yourself creates the foundation for successful relationships.

The Autonomy Paradox

Multiple studies have shown that individuals with a stronger sense of autonomy—those who feel self-directed rather than controlled by others or circumstances—actually form stronger, more interdependent relationships. This creates what researchers call the "autonomy paradox":

The more capable you are of meeting your own psychological needs, the more effectively you can form intimate connections with others.

A 2010 study published in the Journal of Personality and Social Psychology found that individuals with higher autonomy satisfaction:

- Selected partners based on genuine compatibility rather than need fulfilment

- Maintained more explicit boundaries within relationships

- Expressed their authentic feelings and needs more consistently

- Demonstrated greater resilience during relationship challenges

This explains why "needing" a relationship often undermines one's ability to create a healthy one while developing independence counterintuitively increases one's capacity for healthy interdependence.

Self-Determination and Partner Selection

Particularly relevant to dating patterns is research on how self-determination affects partner selection. A longitudinal study by Dr. C. Raymond Knee tracked participants' relationship formations over two years and found that individuals with more decisive self-determination consistently:

1. Selected partners who supported their core values and growth

2. We're less likely to stay in unsatisfying relationships

3. Demonstrated better discrimination between healthy and unhealthy relationship dynamics

4. Showed greater willingness to be single rather than compromise core needs

In contrast, participants with lower self-determination showed patterns of:

1. Selecting partners based on external validation

2. Staying in unsatisfying relationships longer

3. Repeatedly choosing partners who replicated familiar but unhealthy dynamics

4. Demonstrating greater fear of being single

Dr. Knee concluded that developing self-determination is one of the most effective ways to break problematic relationship patterns, as it fundamentally changes both who you're attracted to and what treatment you'll accept.

Competence and Relationship Skills

The competence aspect of Self-Determination Theory helps explain another crucial benefit of developing your self-relationship during a dating sabbatical: you're building relationship skills that transfer directly to romantic connections.

Research by Drs. La Guardia and Patrick examined how competence in emotional self-regulation affected relationship quality. Their findings were striking:

Individuals who developed more excellent skill in:

- Identifying their own emotional needs
- Self-soothing during distress
- Maintaining personal boundaries
- Expressing vulnerability appropriately

Demonstrated significantly higher relationship satisfaction and stability, even when controlling for other factors like compatibility and communication skills.

In essence, by developing competence in relating to yourself during your sabbatical, you're simultaneously building the skills needed for healthy romantic relationships.

Relatedness: The Transfer Effect

Perhaps the most counterintuitive finding from SDT research is what scientists call the "transfer effect" in relatedness. Studies show that how you relate to yourself directly transfers to how you relate to romantic partners.

A groundbreaking study by Dr. Kristin Neff and Dr. S. Natasha Beretvas found that self-compassion was a stronger predictor of healthy relationship behaviors than almost any other factor studied, including:

- Communication training
- Attachment style
- Relationship beliefs

- Previous relationship experiences

Individuals with higher self-compassion:

- Showed greater emotional availability to partners
- Demonstrated more effective conflict resolution
- Were less controlling and critical of partners
- Maintained more precise boundaries in relationships
- Reported higher overall relationship satisfaction

This transfer effect explains why working on your relationship with yourself during a dating sabbatical isn't a distraction from finding love—it's the most direct path to creating it.

The Motivation Continuum and Relationship Patterns

Another valuable insight from SDT research is the motivation continuum, which distinguishes between:

- **Controlled motivation:** Behaving based on external pressure, obligation, or to avoid guilt/shame
- **Autonomous motivation:** Behaving based on personal values, genuine interest, or authentic desire

Studies consistently show that relationships formed and maintained through controlled motivation show higher rates of:

- Conflict and resentment

- Emotional manipulation

- Poor boundary maintenance

- Eventually falling apart or becoming chronically unsatisfying

This research validates a core premise of the Dating Detox: Taking time to clarify your authentic values and desires (autonomous motivation) rather than dating from social pressure or fear of being alone (controlled motivation) dramatically improves your chances of finding lasting fulfilment.

As Dr Ryan noted in a 2019 interview: "Many people approach relationships asking 'What do I need to do or be to find someone?' This controlled motivation actually undermines relationship satisfaction. A more effective question is 'What matters most to me, and how can I create that authentically—both on my own and eventually with a partner?'"

Your dating sabbatical provides the perfect opportunity to transition from controlled to autonomous motivation in your romantic life—a shift that research consistently shows leads to healthier choices and greater fulfilment.

Practical Tool: The Self-Dating Calendar

This tool helps you transform the abstract concept of "dating yourself" into a concrete practice with specific activities to strengthen different aspects of self-relationship.

How It Works

The Self-Dating Calendar involves scheduling regular dates with yourself at three different levels of engagement:

1. **Daily Mini-Dates (5-15 minutes):** Brief but consistent practices that build the habit of attending to your relationship with yourself

2. **Weekly Connection Dates (1-2 hours):** More substantial time dedicated to exploring and developing different aspects of your self-relationship

3. **Monthly Deep Dive Dates (3-4 hours or a full day):** Extended experiences that allow for deeper insight and connection with yourself

The calendar provides structure while allowing flexibility to adapt the specific activities to your preferences and needs.

Setting Up Your Calendar

Start by creating a physical or digital calendar specifically for your self-dating practice. Block out:

- A consistent 5–15-minute period each day for your mini-date

- A 1-2 hour block each week for your connection date

- One more extended block each month for your deep dive date

Treat these appointments with the same respect you would give to dates with someone else. Please put them in your calendar, protect the time, and prepare thoughtfully for them.

Daily Mini-Dates: Building the Foundation

These brief daily practices establish a baseline of attention and care in your relationship with yourself. Choose one focus area each week from the following options:

Week 1: Emotional Awareness

- Morning: "How am I feeling right now? What do I need today?"

- Evening: What emotions arose today? How did I respond to them?"

Week 2: Self-Talk Awareness

- Set 3 random alarms during the day

- When they go off, notice your current self-talk

- If negative, practice a compassionate redirection

Week 3: Needs and Boundaries

- Morning: Identify one need you'll prioritise today

- Evening: Reflect on how well you honoured this need

Week 4: Appreciation Practice

- Morning: Note one quality you appreciate about yourself

- Evening: Identify three things you handled well today

Rebecca, who struggled with harsh self-criticism, found the self-talk awareness practice particularly valuable: "I was shocked by how cruel my internal dialogue was throughout the day. I just noticed it created space to start changing it. By the end of my sabbatical, the voice in my head sounded more like a supportive friend than a hostile critic."

Weekly Connection Dates: Developing the Relationship

These longer sessions allow for deeper exploration and development of your relationship with yourself. Rotate through these categories, choosing one activity each week:

Emotional Connection Dates:

- Journaling session focused on a current emotional challenge

- Creating a physical comfort box with items that soothe each sense

- Practicing a guided self-compassion meditation

- Emotional clearing exercise (safe expression of complicated feelings)

Growth-Focused Dates:

- Learning a new skill, you've been curious about
- Reading a book related to your personal development
- Taking yourself on a "curiosity field trip" to explore a new interest
- Creating a vision board for a specific aspect of your life

Pleasure and Play Dates:

- Engaging in an activity purely because you enjoy it
- Exploring a new form of physical movement that feels good
- Creating something with no purpose beyond creative expression
- Sensory pleasure experience (exceptional food, music, textures)

Rest and Restoration Dates:

- Nature immersion without productivity goals
- Complete digital detox for the duration of the date
- Creating a personal sanctuary space in your home
- Restorative physical practice (gentle yoga, stretching, etc.)

The key is approaching these dates with the same attentiveness you would bring to a date with someone you care about—being fully present, curious, and engaged.

Carlos, who used dating as his primary source of excitement and pleasure, found the weekly dates transformative: "I realised I'd been expecting relationships to be my main source of joy and fulfilment. As I started creating these experiences for myself, I felt less desperate for someone to 'complete' my life."

Monthly Deep Dive Dates: Transformative Experiences

These extended sessions provide opportunities for experiences that can lead to significant shifts in your relationship with yourself. Choose one approach each month:

The Life Review and Visioning Day: Take yourself on a retreat day with your journal to reflect on:

- What's working well in different life areas

- What needs adjustment or renewal

- Clarifying values and priorities for the coming month

- Setting intentions that align with your authentic self

The Self-Connection Adventure: Plan a day-long solo adventure that:

- Takes you somewhere new or meaningful

- Involves elements of both comfort and gentle challenge

- Allows for reflection as well as experience

- Creates memories you can revisit

The Relationship Healing Retreat: Create a personal healing experience focused on:

- Acknowledging a relationship wound you carry

- Exploring how it affects your current patterns

- Creating a symbolic ritual of release or transformation

- Committing to a new way of relating to yourself in this area

The Celebration of Self Day: Design a day dedicated to honouring yourself:

- Activities that highlight your strengths and values

- Experiences that bring you genuine joy

- A self-acknowledgment practice for growth you've achieved

- Creating a meaningful memento of the experience

Mia used her monthly deep dive dates to process grief over past relationships: "I created a ritual where I wrote letters to my past self at different relationship stages, offering the compassion and perspective I didn't have then. It helped me release so much shame and regret I'd been carrying."

Documenting Your Journey

A vital element of the Self-Dating Calendar is documenting your experience. Create a dedicated journal where you record:

- Insights that arise during your dates with yourself
- Changes you notice in how you relate to yourself
- Patterns or themes that emerge across different activities
- Qualities of relationship you're developing with yourself

This documentation serves multiple purposes:

1. It creates accountability for actually doing the practices
2. It helps you recognise growth that might otherwise be subtle
3. It provides a record you can review when old patterns emerge
4. It reinforces your commitment to this relationship

Thomas noticed a surprising pattern in his journal: "I realised I was consistently breaking promises to myself about my weekly dates—rescheduling or shortening them for work obligations. It was a perfect mirror of how I'd been treating my needs in relationships, always putting them last. Seeing it on paper helped me make a conscious change."

From Self-Dating to Partner Dating

As your dating sabbatical progresses and you develop a stronger relationship with yourself, you'll likely notice changes in how you think about future romantic relationships.

Many clients report shifting from viewing potential partners as sources of need fulfilment to seeing them as people with whom they might create something meaningful while remaining complete in themselves.

Elena described this shift eloquently: "Before my sabbatical, my unspoken question on dates was always 'Will this person make me feel worthy and complete?' Now I find myself wondering, 'Could we create something beautiful together while supporting each other's wholeness?' It's a completely different starting point."

This perspective transformation doesn't happen overnight. It emerges gradually through consistent practice of relating to yourself in the ways you hope to eventually relate to a partner—with attention, care, respect, and genuine curiosity.

CHAPTER 6:

Healing Your Relationship with Love

Processing Past Relationship Trauma

Let's be real: by the time most of us reach adulthood, our hearts look less like pristine organs and more like vintage leather jackets—worn in places, patched up in others, with a few questionable stains we can't quite explain. This isn't a bad thing! Character comes from living, and living inevitably involves some heartache (and maybe a few regrettable Tinder dates).

However, there's a crucial difference between a heart that has been through some things and emerged stronger versus one that is still carrying active wounds that turn every new relationship into an episode of "Dating Horror Stories." The former has integrated past hurts into wisdom; the latter continues to bleed onto everyone it touches—which, trust me, is *not* a great first date strategy.

During your dating sabbatical, one of your most important tasks is healing your relationship with love itself. Because here's the truth: you don't just have relationships with people. You have a relationship with the very concept of love, and that relationship might currently be giving love the silent treatment while scrolling through its texts.

How Past Wounds Become Present Patterns

Think of your earliest experiences with love as the foundation upon which all your later romantic experiences are built. If that foundation includes significant cracks (or, let's be honest, entire missing walls), everything built on top of it will reflect those issues—no matter how many throw pillows and fancy candles you add to the décor.

This happens through what psychologists call "internalized working models"—mental templates created from early attachment experiences that operate like relationship autopilot. It's like having a GPS that's determined to route you through every emotional pothole in town.

When these working models form around painful experiences, they create distortions in how you experience love:

- Betrayal becomes expected rather than surprising

- Conditional love feels more "real" than unconditional acceptance

- Drama registers as passion, while stability feels boring (or as I like to call it, "Netflix and Actually Chill")

- Emotional unavailability seems normal, while genuine availability feels suspicious

Maya realized her working model of love was built around earning affection rather than receiving it freely. "My father's attention was always conditional on achievement," she explained. "I recreated this dynamic in every relationship, constantly performing for approval rather than simply being myself. Dating me was basically like watching a one-woman show called 'Please Love Me: The Musical' every night."

Understanding these connections doesn't immediately heal them, but it does make visible what was previously operating in the shadows. This visibility is the necessary first step toward transformation—like turning on the lights to see what's been making that weird noise in your emotional basement.

The Physical Reality of Emotional Wounds

Relationship trauma isn't just psychological—it's physiological. Research by Dr. Bessel van der Kolk and others demonstrates that emotional wounds create physical patterns in your nervous system and brain:

- Neural pathways form around threat detection specific to your relationship wounds

- Your autonomic nervous system becomes primed to anticipate similar injuries

- Protective responses (fight/flight/freeze/fawn) activate more quickly and intensely

- Psychological defenses deploy automatically to prevent re-experiencing past pain

These physical realities explain why "just getting over it" or "thinking more positively" rarely resolves relationship trauma. The wounds live in your body as much as in your mind, and healing requires approaches that address both. It's like trying to fix your car by just talking sternly to it—sometimes you actually need to get under the hood.

Jason, a financial analyst who prided himself on rational thinking, was frustrated by his inability to "logic his way out" of his fear of abandonment. "I kept telling myself the patterns were irrational, but my body wouldn't listen," he shared. "I'd still wake up in a panic when someone took too long to respond to a text. My brain would say 'They're probably just busy,' while my body was staging a full-on production of 'They're Definitely Ghosting You: The Sequel.'"

Through body-based healing practices, Jason gradually rewired these physiological responses. "I had to speak the language my nervous system understood—sensation, breath, and movement—not just cognitive reframing. Turns out my amygdala doesn't respond well to PowerPoint presentations on why I shouldn't be anxious."

Forgiving Others (and Yourself)

People tend to have strong reactions when discussing forgiving past partners or past relationship injuries. Some view forgiveness as a form of spiritual bypassing or letting someone "off the hook" for their harmful behavior. Others view it as a moral imperative regardless of circumstances. They're both a little right and a little wrong, like most heated debates about emotional matters.

Let's clarify what forgiveness means in the context of healing your relationship with love:

What Forgiveness Is (and isn't)

Forgiveness IS:

- Releasing yourself from the burden of carrying resentment (because that baggage is WAY over the airline limit)

- Accepting what happened without continuing to fight against reality

- Reclaiming energy previously devoted to anger or bitterness

- Creating space for new experiences uncoloured by past wounds

Forgiveness IS NOT:

- Condoning hurtful behaviour or saying it was acceptable

- Requiring reconciliation or renewed trust

- Denying the impact or significance of what happened

- A one-time decision rather than an ongoing process

Think of forgiveness as a gift you give yourself, not the person who hurt you. It's about freedom from the past, not approval of it. It's like unfriending someone in real life—they don't get a notification, but you get peace.

Tanya struggled to forgive her ex, who had shattered her trust. "I kept thinking forgiveness meant what he did was okay, which it wasn't," she explained. "The breakthrough came when I realised forgiveness wasn't about him—it was about not letting that experience determine my future. I wasn't declaring his actions 'Certified Fresh' on Rotten Tomatoes; I was refusing to let him be the director of my next relationship."

Self-Forgiveness: The Often-Overlooked Key

While much attention goes to forgiving others, forgiving yourself is equally crucial—and often more challenging. Self-forgiveness involves releasing shame and self-punishment around:

- Choices you made that led to painful outcomes

- Red flags you missed or ignored (even those red flags so big they could have been seen from space)

- Ways you compromised your values or boundaries

- Patterns you continued despite knowing better

- Time you feel you "wasted" in unsuitable relationships (those three years with someone who thought deodorant was "optional")

Self-forgiveness is not about absolving yourself of responsibility but about approaching your past self with the same compassion you would offer a good friend doing their best with the awareness, tools, and healing they had at the time.

Carlos felt immense shame about repeatedly choosing partners who mistreated him. "I kept thinking, 'I should have known better,'" he shared. "The turning point was realising that past-me wasn't deliberately making bad choices—he was unconsciously seeking what felt familiar from childhood. He needed understanding, not judgment. Past-me was working with an outdated user manual for relationships; he wasn't deliberately downloading emotional viruses."

The Forgiveness Process: Practical Steps

Forgiveness isn't a feeling that magically appears—it's a practice you cultivate through specific actions. It's less "bibbidi-bobbidi-boo" and more "wax on, wax off."

1. Acknowledge the Full Impact

Before moving toward forgiveness, fully acknowledge what happened and its effects on you:

- Write out the complete story of the relationship injury

- Name the specific impacts it had on you emotionally, mentally, and physically

- Identify how the experience has shaped your beliefs about love and relationships

- Allow yourself to feel the emotions associated with the experience

Rushing past this step often leads to incomplete healing. You can't truly forgive what you haven't fully acknowledged. It's like trying to clean a spill without admitting there's something sticky on the floor.

2. Separate Facts from Interpretations

Distinguish between what objectively happened and the meaning you assigned to it:

- "They stopped calling" is a fact; "They stopped calling because I'm unlovable" is an interpretation

- "The relationship ended" is a fact; "The relationship ended because I'm flawed" is an interpretation

- "They chose someone else" is a fact; "They chose someone else because I wasn't enough" is an interpretation

This separation helps you recognise where you may be carrying unnecessary pain through meaning-making that extends beyond what occurred. Your brain loves to play detective and solve mysteries, even when it has to make up the crime.

3. Identify What You've Learned

Extract the wisdom and growth from painful experiences:

- What did this experience teach you about your needs and boundaries?

- What relationship skills did you develop as a result?

- How did this experience clarify your values or non-negotiables?

- What strengths did you discover in yourself through the challenge?

Finding value in painful experiences doesn't justify the pain but does help transform it from meaningless suffering into meaningful growth. It's taking emotional lemons and making something stronger than lemonade—maybe emotional whiskey.

4. Practice Forgiveness Rituals

Create symbolic experiences that concretise your forgiveness process:

- Write a letter to the person who hurt you (not to send) expressing everything you've held back

- Create a forgiveness ceremony where you symbolically release the burden

- Develop a daily practice of consciously choosing to set down resentment

- Use visualisation to imagine cutting energetic cords that connect you to the past injury

Elena created a powerful ritual where she wrote all her resentments toward her ex on dissolving paper, then placed it in water and watched it disappear. "There was something powerful about physically watching the words disappear, which helped my mind accept that it was time to let go. Plus, it was way more satisfying than just deleting their number for the fifteenth time."

5. Develop a Compassion Practice

Cultivate compassion toward yourself and others involved:

- Practice seeing the humanity in the person who hurt you (without excusing their actions)

- Acknowledge the wounded parts of them that contributed to their harmful behaviour

- Offer compassion to the part of yourself that experienced the pain

- Extend understanding to the part of yourself that may have contributed to the dynamic

This compassion practice isn't about assigning blame but recognising the complex humanity in all relationships—even painful ones. We're all just walking around with our emotional baggage, occasionally bumping into each other in the terminal.

The Freedom of Release

The ultimate goal of forgiveness is freedom—liberation from carrying past relationship wounds into your present and future. This freedom manifests as:

- The ability to tell your story without being emotionally hijacked by it

- Decreased physiological reactivity to triggers related to the wound

- Greater discernment in relationships without hypervigilance or paranoia

- The capacity to be fully present with new connections rather than seeing them through the lens of past injuries

This freedom doesn't typically emerge as a sudden transformation but gradually emerges through consistent practice and patience. It's less like flipping a light switch and more like watching a sunrise—you can't pinpoint the exact moment darkness becomes light, but eventually, the difference is undeniable.

Rebuilding Trust in the Process of Love

Beyond healing specific relationship wounds, many people need to rebuild trust in the very process of love and connection. After disappointment or heartbreak, it's common to develop mistrust toward potential partners and love itself.

Signs you might have developed mistrust in the process of love include:

- Believing lasting love exists for others but not for you (like WiFi that works in every apartment but yours)

- Expecting disappointment even when things are going well

- Feeling that genuine connection is rare or impossible to maintain

- Approaching dating with cynicism rather than open-hearted hope

- Believing that vulnerability inevitably leads to pain

This mistrust creates a self-fulfilling prophecy: When you don't trust the process of love, you engage with it guardedly, which makes authentic connection less likely. This then reinforces your belief that love doesn't work. Breaking this cycle requires rebuilding trust in others and in love itself—like relearning to swim after getting caught in a riptide.

Reclaiming Your Capacity for Connection

External forces cannot permanently damage your ability to love and be loved unless you allow them to. It's an innate capacity that may be temporarily obscured by pain but never destroyed. Your heart comes with a lifetime warranty; it just needs some maintenance.

Reclaiming this capacity involves:

1. Challenging Love-Limiting Beliefs

Identify and question the restrictive beliefs you've adopted about love:

- "All relationships eventually disappoint."
- "The more I care, the more I'll get hurt."
- "Real connection is rare or impossible."
- "I'll never find someone who accepts all of me." (Including your collection of rubber ducks or your ability to quote entire episodes of The Office)

For each belief, ask:

- Is this statement always true?
- What evidence might contradict this belief?

- How is holding this belief affecting my experience of connection?

- What might be possible if I didn't hold this belief?

2. Creating Evidence for New Beliefs

Actively seek experiences that provide evidence for more hopeful beliefs:

- Notice and document moments of genuine connection (romantic or not)

- Pay attention to examples of healthy, lasting love around you

- Create small opportunities to experience being seen and valued

- Practice vulnerability in low-risk situations to build evidence that it doesn't always lead to pain

Marcus began keeping what he called a "love evidence journal," documenting moments of genuine connection he observed or experienced. "After a few months, I had pages of evidence that real love exists. Maintaining my cynicism when confronted with all these examples made it harder. It was like trying to claim pizza isn't delicious while surrounded by people enjoying pizza."

3. Embracing the Risk of Hope

Ultimately, loving requires courage—the willingness to hope despite disappointment. This means:

- Acknowledging that, yes, opening your heart involves risk

- Recognizing that protecting yourself from all possibility of pain also blocks joy

- Choosing to be brave enough to hope again, not because it's guaranteed to work out but because a life without that courage is too limited

This isn't naive optimism but clear-eyed courage—seeing the potential for pain and beauty and choosing to remain open to connection anyway. It's like returning to the emotional roller coaster even though you threw up last time—because the thrill is worth it.

Exercise: The Letter You'll Never Send

This powerful exercise helps process relationship wounds by creating space for full emotional expression, free from the limitations of actual communication. It combines written catharsis with intentional release to support healing. Think of it as texting your ex after a bottle of wine—but therapeutic and without the morning-after regrets.

Step 1: Choose Your Recipient

Decide who needs to receive this unsent letter. Options include:

- A specific ex-partner who hurt you significantly
- A composite of several past partners who treated you similarly
- Your past self at a particular relationship stage
- The concept of love itself

Choose the recipient whose role in your relationship wounds feels most active or unresolved.

Step 2: Create a Safe Space

Create a private and comfortable environment where you can express yourself fully without concern about being interrupted or overheard. Have tissues nearby—emotional release is often a natural consequence of this exercise. And maybe chocolate. Chocolate helps everything.

Step 3: Write Without Censorship

Begin writing to your chosen recipient, expressing everything you've held back:

- Start with "I need you to know..." or "I never told you..."
- Express your anger, hurt, and disappointment without filtering

- Include specific incidents and how they affected you
- Share what you needed that you didn't receive
- Express regrets or things you wish had happened differently
- Include any positive acknowledgements if they feel authentic
- End with what you need to say to feel complete

This letter is intended for your healing, so please be completely honest. Write until you feel complete—this might be two pages or twenty. Consider it the director's cut of your emotional experience—no time limits, no commercials.

Step 4: The Intentional Release

After completing your letter, create a ritualised release:

- Read it aloud as if the recipient could hear you
- Then choose a release method:
    - Burning the letter safely and watching it transform
    - Tearing it into tiny pieces
    - Burying it in the earth
    - Dissolving it in water

As you release the physical letter, visualise releasing the emotional burden it represents. It's like Marie Kondo-ing your emotional clutter—thank it for its service and let it go.

Step 5: Self-Compassion Closure

After the release, place a hand on your heart and speak these words (or your version) aloud: "I honour the pain I've carried and the courage it took to express it. I am now choosing to release what no longer serves me. This experience is part of my story but does not define my future."

The Impact of Emotional Release

Sophia described her experience with this exercise: "I wrote twelve pages to my ex who had betrayed my trust. I poured out my rage, heartbreak, and things I'd been too afraid to admit even to myself. When I burned the letter, I felt its weight leaving my body. The betrayal still occurred, but its power over me had dramatically diminished. I finally stopped mentally rehearsing witty comebacks for a confrontation that would never happen."

This exercise may need to be repeated several times for significant wounds, with each iteration often reaching more profound layers of the experience. Some people find that subsequent letters become shorter as the emotional charge diminishes—like wringing out a sponge until it dries.

Expert Interviews: Trauma Specialists on Relationship Healing

To provide deeper insight into healing relationship wounds, I spoke with several specialists in relationship trauma recovery. Here are key perspectives from these conversations:

Dr. Jessica Chen, a Psychologist Specializing in Attachment Trauma

The connection between past and present: "The relationships that hurt us most become templates for future connections unless we consciously intervene. This isn't just psychological—it's neurobiological. Your brain creates neural pathways based on relationship experiences, creating a superhighway toward familiar, painful relationships.

The good news is that neuroplasticity works both ways. The same brain that learns to expect pain in relationships can also learn to expect safety, but this requires consistent new experiences that contradict the old pattern. It's like retraining a dog taught to fear the mailman."

On practical healing approaches: "Combining cognitive understanding with somatic (body-based) approaches is most effective for relationship healing. Understanding the 'why' behind your patterns creates context, but true transformation requires engaging with the nervous system where the trauma is stored.

Simple practices like learning to track bodily sensations during relationship triggers, developing personalised self-regulation techniques, and gradually expanding your 'window of tolerance' for intimacy can dramatically reshape your capacity for healthy connection. Your body needs to experience safety, not just hear about it."

Marco Rivera, LMFT, Specialist in Relationship Pattern Transformation

"The biggest misconception about forgiveness is that it's primarily about the other person. In my practice, I define forgiveness as 'releasing yourself from the prison of resentment.' It's not about condoning harmful behaviour but about freeing yourself from the emotional burden of what happened.

Many clients resist forgiveness because they believe it means saying what happened was okay. I help them see that forgiveness says, 'What happened matters—and I'm choosing not to let it control my future.' It's like refusing to let your ex continue to occupy your emotional apartment rent-free."

On the stages of healing: "Relationship healing typically follows a pattern: destabilisation as old wounds are acknowledged, followed by a period of integration that can feel messy and nonlinear, and finally reorganisation around new, healthier patterns.

Many people get discouraged in the middle stage because it doesn't feel like evident progress. I remind clients that healing isn't a straight line—it's more like a spiral in which they revisit similar themes from progressively healthier perspectives. It's like cleaning out your garage—sometimes it looks messier halfway through the process than when you started, but that's part of getting organised."

Dr. Aisha Johnson, Trauma-Informed Relationship Coach

On rebuilding trust capacity: "After relationship trauma, many people focus exclusively on determining who is trustworthy; however, equally important is rebuilding your trust capacity—your ability to trust appropriately and recover when that trust is occasionally misplaced.

I work with clients to develop 'resilient trust'—the ability to connect with discernment rather than naive openness or defensive closure. This resilient trust includes knowing you can survive disappointment if it occurs, which paradoxically makes you more capable of authentic connection. It's like having emotional health insurance—you hope you won't need it, but knowing it's there lets you take reasonable risks."

On post-traumatic relationship growth: "While we're familiar with the concept of post-traumatic stress, I focus on post-traumatic growth—the ways relationship wounds, when healed, can become sources of wisdom, compassion, and more profound capacity for connection.

When clients integrate their painful experiences rather than just trying to get over them, they often develop greater emotional intelligence, clearer boundaries, more authentic communication skills, and more profound empathy—all qualities that support healthier future relationships. It's turning relationship lemons into emotional lemonade with a kick."

Research Spotlight: Post-Traumatic Relationship Growth

While much attention goes to the damaging effects of relationship trauma, emerging research explores the concept of post-traumatic relationship growth. These positive psychological changes can appear following the struggle with highly challenging relationship experiences. Yes, that's right—your terrible ex might accidentally make you awesome.

The Science of Growth After Relationship Pain

A 2018 Journal of Family Psychology meta-analysis examined outcomes following relationship trauma across 42 studies. The researchers found that while relationship wounds initially create distress, approximately 65% of individuals eventually reported positive changes, including:

1. **Enhanced Discernment**: Sharpened ability to recognise relationship patterns and select compatible partners

2. **Increased Self-Knowledge**: A deeper understanding of personal needs, boundaries, and values

3. **Improved Emotional Intelligence**: Greater skill in identifying, expressing, and managing emotions

4. **Stronger Boundaries**: A clearer sense of acceptable and unacceptable treatment

5. **Deeper Capacity for Intimacy**: Ability to connect more authentically after healing defensive patterns

These findings align with broader post-traumatic growth research suggesting that struggling with difficult experiences can ultimately expand your psychological resources and capacities—if the experiences are metabolised rather than just endured. It's like emotional weight training—the resistance creates the strength.

Factors That Promote Post-Traumatic Relationship Growth

Research by Drs. Calhoun and Tedeschi, pioneers in post-traumatic growth research, identified key factors that determine whether people experience growth following relationship trauma:

1. **Processing vs. Rumination** Studies distinguish between productive processing (making meaning of experiences) and unproductive rumination (repetitive negative thinking). Those who engaged in deliberate processing showed significantly higher growth outcomes than those who ruminated or avoided processing altogether. There's a difference between reflecting on your past and just replaying it like your favourite sad song on repeat.

2. **Narrative Development** Research shows that creating a coherent narrative about relationship wounds—acknowledging pain while integrating it into a larger life story—strongly predicts growth. This narrative development transforms fragmented traumatic memories into meaningful experiences. You're the author of your story, not just a character in someone else's.

3. **Social Support Quality** The nature of support following relationship trauma significantly impacts growth potential. Studies show that validation (acknowledging the reality of the experience) combined with gentle encouragement toward meaning-making creates optimal conditions for growth. The right friends will both validate your pain AND gently prevent you from texting your ex at 2 AM.

4. **Meaning-Making Opportunities** Research demonstrates that structured opportunities to derive meaning from painful experiences—whether through therapy, writing exercises, or guided reflection—

dramatically increase the likelihood of post-traumatic growth. Don't just survive it—make it mean something.

5. **Self-Compassion Practice** Multiple studies have identified self-compassion as a crucial mediator between trauma and growth. Those who respond to their suffering with kindness rather than judgment are significantly more likely to experience positive transformation. Talk to yourself like you're your own best friend, not like you're a disappointed parent.

Application to Your Dating Sabbatical

This research offers encouraging evidence that your relationship wounds can become sources of wisdom and growth during your dating sabbatical. To leverage these findings:

- Engage in structured processing of past relationship experiences through journaling, therapy, or guided exercises

- Develop a coherent narrative about your relationship history that acknowledges both pain and learning

- Seek quality support that validates your experience while encouraging growth

- Create specific opportunities to derive meaning from painful experiences

- Practice self-compassion as you move through the healing process

Remember: The goal isn't to be grateful for painful experiences but to honour your resilience in moving through them and to recognise how they've expanded your capacity for genuine connection.

As you continue your dating sabbatical, approach the healing process as recovering what was damaged and developing new capacities that weren't present. When fully processed, your relationship wounds can become the foundation for a deeper, more authentic connection in the future. Like a broken bone that heals stronger at the fracture point, your heart can become more resilient precisely where it was once broken.

CHAPTER 7:

Building Your Support System

The Role of Community in Healthy Dating

If there's one misconception that romantic comedies have sold us more effectively than any other, it's this: your romantic partner should be your everything. Your lover, best friend, therapist, life coach, primary emotional support, and sole adventure companion—all wrapped into one convenient (and impossibly attractive) package with perfect hair even at 6 AM.

We see it in the classic rom-com finale: two people finally get together, and suddenly, they're complete, riding off into the sunset with no friends or family members in sight. Roll the credits! Who needs anyone else when you've found "The One," right? (Spoiler alert: you do.)

This isolation narrative isn't just unrealistic—it's a blueprint for relationship disaster. It's like expecting one houseplant to transform your entire apartment into a lush jungle. It's not going to happen, my friend.

The truth is that the healthiest romantic relationships exist within a web of other meaningful connections. The idea that one person should meet all your social and emotional needs isn't just unfair to them—it's about as sustainable as trying to live on nothing but chocolate cake. It's delicious at first, but you'll have problems down the road.

The Pressure Cooker of Romantic Isolation

When you rely on a romantic partner as your primary or only source of emotional support and connection, you create what relationship therapists call a "pressure cooker" dynamic (and unlike your Instant Pot, this pressure doesn't result in a delicious dinner):

1. Your partner can't possibly fulfil all your connection needs, leading to inevitable disappointment

2. Normal relationship fluctuations feel catastrophic because there's no support buffer

3. The fear of losing your sole support person makes healthy boundary-setting nearly impossible

4. The relationship becomes a pressure cooker where tensions have nowhere else to vent

Jessica experienced this firsthand when she moved to a new city for her boyfriend's job. "I had no friends or connections there, so he became my entire world," she explained. "When we hit a rough patch, I completely fell apart because I had no other emotional outlets. My desperation to fix things actually pushed him further away—turns out, being someone's entire universe feels less like a compliment and more like being trapped in a very clingy black hole."

During her dating sabbatical, Jessica prioritised building her community. "By the time I started dating again, I had formed a running group, a book club, and two close friends with whom I spoke weekly. Dating from that place felt completely different—I chose partners from a place of desire rather than desperate need. It's amazing how much more attractive you are when you're not silently screaming 'PLEASE COMPLETE ME' on first dates."

The Research on Relationship Sustainability

The importance of community isn't just anecdotal—it's backed by solid research (because nothing says romance like peer-reviewed studies):

- A longitudinal study from the University of Texas found that couples with diverse social networks experienced greater relationship longevity than those who were socially isolated.

- Research by relationship psychologist Dr Terry Orbuch revealed that women with strong friendships outside their romantic relationships reported significantly higher marital satisfaction.

- A study published in the Journal of Social and Personal Relationships found that couples who maintained individual friendships alongside couple friendships showed greater resilience during relationship challenges.

The conclusion is clear: having a support network beyond your romantic relationship doesn't threaten your connection—it strengthens it by removing unsustainable pressure and providing perspective during inevitable challenging periods. Think of it as relationship insurance that actually pays dividends.

The Foundation Triangle: Self, Community, Partner

Rather than the traditional model where partners are expected to be everything to each other (a job description that would make even Superman update his resume), consider what I call the "Foundation Triangle":

1. **Relationship with Self**: Your core emotional regulation, identity, and personal fulfilment

2. **Relationship with Community**: Your web of friendships, family connections, and social supports

3. **Relationship with Partner**: Your romantic connection, built upon the stability of the other two sides

This triangle provides stability that a single connection point cannot. When your romantic relationship experiences everyday stress or conflict, you can maintain emotional balance and perspective through your relationships with yourself and your community.

This balanced model also ensures that people enter and maintain relationships voluntarily rather than out of desperate need—one of the strongest predictors of relationship satisfaction. After all, there's a big difference between "I want you" and "I'll literally wither and die without you." One is romantic; the other belongs in a gothic novel.

Creating Accountability

One of the most valuable functions of a support system during and after your dating sabbatical is accountability—helping you maintain your commitment to healthier patterns when old habits inevitably try to reassert themselves. Think of them as your dating GPS, recalculating when you turn wrong toward Heartbreak Hotel.

Why You Need Dating Accountability Partners

Even with the best intentions and most straightforward insights, changing entrenched dating patterns is challenging. Your brain has developed neural superhighways toward certain behaviours and responses, and these old pathways remain even as you build new ones. It's like your brain has a favourite coffee shop it visits on autopilot, even though it knows there's a better one just around the corner.

Accountability partners help in several crucial ways:

1. **External perspective**: They can see your patterns more objectively than you can (like noticing that "spontaneous" is your code word for "emotionally unavailable")

2. **Pattern interruption**: They can call attention to behaviours you might not notice

3. **Commitment reinforcement**: Stating your intentions to someone else significantly increases follow-through

4. **Celebration support**: They acknowledge the progress you might minimise or overlook

5. **Reality checking**: They help distinguish between authentic connection and familiar-but-unhealthy dynamics (or as I like to call it, "same trash, different packaging")

Research in behaviour change shows that people with structured accountability are up to 95% more likely to achieve their goals than those working on change alone. This applies particularly to changes in relationship patterns, where our rose-coloured glasses have an annoying tendency to slip back on without us noticing.

Selecting the Right Accountability Partners

Not everyone in your life is suited to be a dating accountability partner. The ideal candidates have:

1. **Direct communication style**: They're willing to speak brutal truths compassionately (not the friend who says "He seemed nice" about literally everyone, including your ex who "borrowed" your credit card)

2. **Pattern recognition**: They've observed your dating history and can identify recurring dynamics

3. **Healthy relationship understanding**: They have evidence of healthy relationship knowledge in their own lives

4. **Appropriate boundaries**: They respect your autonomy while providing honest feedback

5. **Accessibility**: They're consistently available for check-ins when needed

Consider diversifying your accountability team with different perspectives:

- A long-time friend who knows your history
- A newer friend who sees you with fresh eyes
- A family member who understands your background
- A therapist or coach with a professional perspective
- A peer who's doing similar relationship work

Carlos created his "dating board of directors"—three friends with different strengths who helped him maintain his new relationship approach. "My friend Mark calls me out when I start rationalising red flags, Sarah helps me process emotions without acting impulsively, and Jordan celebrates progress with me. Having different perspectives keeps me balanced. It's like having a relationship with the Avengers team—each with their own superpower to help save me from myself."

Structured Accountability That Works

Vague accountability rarely creates change. Instead, establish specific structures:

1. The Pre-Date Advisory

Before returning to dating, meet with your accountability partners to:

- Review the insights from your sabbatical
- Identify specific patterns you're committed to changing

- Establish concrete recognition signals for old patterns

- Create communication protocols for when you need support

2. The Regular Check-In System

Schedule consistent check-ins rather than waiting for problems:

- Weekly brief updates during active dating periods

- Monthly more profound reflection sessions

- Immediate access protocol for high-risk situations (like when you're tempted to text "u up?" at 1 AM to that ex who was bad news)

3. The Pattern Intervention Agreement

Create explicit permission for intervention when old patterns emerge:

- Specific language accountability partners can use

- Agreement on how you'll receive feedback

- Commitment to pause and reflect before defensive responses

4. The Progress Tracking Method

Establish how you'll measure and celebrate progress:

- Specific behaviours that indicate pattern changes

- Recognition of internal shifts as well as external actions

- Regular acknowledgement of growth, even amid occasional setbacks

Rachel and her accountability partner Sarah developed a colour-coded system: "Green means things are on track with healthy patterns. Yellow means I'm noticing old tendencies emerging. Red means I'm actively sliding into old patterns and need immediate support. This simple framework makes asking for the right help at the right time easier. It's like a weather alert system, but for my dating climate. 'Caution: High chance of terrible decisions tonight. Seek shelter immediately.'"

Selecting Dating Mentors and Advisors

Beyond accountability partners who help you maintain your commitments, dating mentors and advisors provide wisdom, guidance, and examples of healthy relationships. Think of them as your relationship, Yodas, minus the confusing syntax.

The Power of Relationship Models

We learn how to be in relationships primarily by observing others. If you didn't have healthy relationship models growing up, actively selecting mentors now can fill that gap and provide templates for what's possible.

Effective relationship mentors:

- Demonstrate the kind of relationship dynamic you aspire to create

- Have navigated challenges similar to the ones you face

- Communicate openly about both the joys and difficulties of their relationships

- Maintain appropriate boundaries while sharing valuable insights

- Offer perspective without imposing their path as the only right one

These mentors might be:

- Couples in your community whose relationships you admire

- Family members with healthy long-term partnerships

- Professional counsellors with relationship expertise

- Thought leaders whose work on relationships resonates with you

- Friends slightly ahead of you on their relationship healing journey

Tanya deliberately sought mentorship from her colleague, Maria, and her husband, who had a balanced, supportive relationship she hoped to create. "I asked if I could occasionally take them to dinner and ask questions about their relationship. Their willingness to share their successes and struggles gave me a real-world picture of what a healthy partnership looks like on a day-to-day basis. Even the healthiest couples occasionally fight about whose turn it is to clean the bathroom—they don't threaten to burn down the house when they do it."

Learning from Different Relationship Stages

When selecting relationship mentors, include people at different relationship stages:

1. **The New Relationship Navigators**: People who are successfully implementing healthy patterns in newer relationships

2. **The Mid-Journey Maintainers**: Couples who have moved beyond the honeymoon phase and are actively nurturing their connection

3. **The Long-Term Thrivers**: Partnerships that have weathered significant life challenges while maintaining the connection

4. **The Conscious Uncouplers**: People who have ended relationships with maturity and growth rather than destruction (yes, even breakups can be done well, despite what social media and your Spotify breakup playlist might suggest)

This diversity offers a unique perspective on how healthy relationships evolve across various phases and challenges.

Creating Mentorship Structures That Work

Relationship mentorship is most effective when it operates within clear structures rather than relying on vague intentions.

The Specific Question Approach: Rather than general advice-seeking, prepare specific questions:

- "How do you navigate differences in communication styles?"

- "What practices help you maintain connection during busy periods?"

- "How have you evolved your relationship agreements over time?"

The Observation Period: Sometimes, watching healthy relationships in action teaches more than direct advice:

- Spend time with couples whose dynamics you admire

- Notice how they communicate, resolve disagreements, and support each other

- Identify specific behaviours you might adapt to your style

The Case Study Method: Present specific relationship situations to your mentors:

- Describe a pattern or challenge you're experiencing

- Ask how they might approach this situation

- Listen for principles rather than seeking exact formulas

The Reverse Mentorship: Consider what you might offer in return:

- Skills or knowledge in your areas of expertise
- Perspective from your generation or background
- Assistance with projects or challenges they face

Jordan created quarterly "relationship wisdom dinners" where he invited couples he admired for specific reasons. "I would focus each dinner on a theme, such as communication, maintaining individuality, or navigating family dynamics. Having multiple perspectives in the room showed me that there is no right way to create a healthy relationship—just principles that can be expressed in different styles. Plus, people love talking about their relationships almost as much as complaining about their jobs, so getting them to participate was surprisingly easy."

Exercise: Mapping Your Support Network

To intentionally build your relationship support system, start by mapping your current network and identifying areas for development. Don't worry—unlike most exercises, this one doesn't involve burpees or sweating through your favourite shirt.

Step 1: Assess Your Current Support System

Draw a circle representing yourself in the centre of a page. Then, map your existing relationships in concentric circles based on closeness and connection type:

- Inner Circle: People you currently trust with vulnerability and regular contact.

- Middle Circle: Regular connections with moderate emotional sharing.

- Outer Circle: Occasional connections or specific contexts only.

Within each circle, use different colours or symbols to indicate:

- People who give you honest feedback versus those who mainly affirm

- People who have healthy relationship knowledge versus those with limited perspective

- People who are consistently available versus sporadically accessible

- People who know your relationship history versus those with limited context

This visual mapping helps identify strengths and gaps in your current support network. It might also reveal that your cat, while adorable, is not providing you with actionable dating advice.

Step 2: Identify Network Needs

Based on your map, identify what's missing from your current support system:

- Do you have enough people who will tell you brutal truths?

- Do you have connections with people in healthy relationships?

- Do you have diverse perspectives and experiences?

- Do you have support available at various times and in different contexts?

- Do you have professional support in addition to personal connections?

Create a specific list of the types of support you need to add to your network.

Step 3: Develop Your Network Expansion Plan

For each identified need, create an action plan:

For Deepening Existing Connections:

- Which current relationships could develop into more substantial support?

- What specific conversations would help evolve these relationships?

- What reciprocal support could you offer to nurture these connections?

For Creating New Connections:

- What communities, groups, or contexts might contain potential supporters?

- What initial steps would introduce you to these potential connections?

- How will you communicate your desire for an authentic relationship?

For Professional Support:

- What type of professional guidance would complement your network?

- What qualifications or approach would best serve your specific needs?

- What practical constraints (location, budget, schedule) must be considered?

Step 4: Create Your Support Protocol

Develop clear guidance for how and when you'll engage your support system:

Regular Connection Schedule:

- Weekly check-ins with primary accountability partners

- Monthly deeper conversations with mentors

- Quarterly review of your overall support network effectiveness

Situation-Specific Protocols:

- Who to contact when experiencing strong attraction to potentially unhealthy dynamics

- Who to consult before making significant relationship decisions

- Who to reach out to after difficult dating experiences

Communication Guidelines:

- How you'll ask for different types of support (listening, advice, perspective)

- How you'll receive feedback, especially when it's challenging

- How you'll express gratitude and reciprocate support

Maya created a simple yet effective support protocol: "I have three designated people I text 'Code Red' when I'm tempted to contact my ex or pursue someone with familiar red flags. They know exactly what this means and respond with pre-planned reality-checking questions. This system has prevented me from reverting to old patterns numerous times. It's like having a dating version of poison control on speed dial—emergency support when I'm about to ingest something toxic."

Research Spotlight: Social Network Effects on Relationship Quality

The importance of social support for relationship health isn't just intuitive—it's backed by extensive research. Let's examine what science reveals about the impact of social networks on romantic relationships (warning: science ahead, but I promise to keep it painless).

The Predictive Power of Social Integration

Multiple longitudinal studies demonstrate that couples' level of social integration—their connectedness to friends, family, and community—significantly predicts relationship quality and longevity:

- Research by Drs. Karney and Bradbury found that couples with diverse social connections showed greater resilience during relationship stressors than socially isolated couples.

- A 10-year study from the University of Michigan revealed that couples with stronger community ties reported higher relationship satisfaction and lower divorce rates than those with limited social networks.

- Dr. Terri Orbuch's research demonstrated that women with close friendships outside their marriages reported 40% higher marital satisfaction than those who relied primarily on their husbands for emotional support.

These findings suggest that building your social network isn't just personally fulfilling—it's a direct investment in your future relationship health. Who knew that maintaining your Thursday night book club might be relationship insurance?

The Opinion Effect: How Networks Shape Partner Selection

Research by Dr. Benjamin Karney and colleagues reveals that our social networks significantly influence both whom we select as partners and how those relationships develop:

- Approval from friends and family predicted relationship longevity more accurately than the couple's satisfaction reports in the early stages of the relationship.

- Couples who received positive feedback about their relationship from their social networks were likelier to progress toward commitment than those who received mixed or negative feedback.

- When social networks expressed reservations about a relationship, people were more likely to notice problems they had previously overlooked.

This "opinion effect" means your support network doesn't just help you maintain healthy patterns—it actively shapes your perception of potential partners, often noticing compatibility issues or red flags before you consciously recognize them. It's like having relationship security cameras installed in your blind spots.

The Buffer Effect: How Support Systems Protect Relationships

Psychology research has identified what's called the "buffer effect," where strong social networks act as protective barriers during relationship challenges:

- Studies show that couples with robust support systems experience the same stressors as other couples but report less relationship damage from these stressors.

- Research by Dr Katherine Fiori found that different types of social support (emotional, practical, informational) each contributed uniquely to relationship resilience.

- A study published in the Journal of Family Psychology demonstrated that support from friends reduced physiological stress responses during couple conflicts, promoting healthier communication.

This research explains why isolated couples often experience more relationship damage from the same challenges that socially connected couples navigate successfully—they lack the stress-buffering effect that diverse support provides. It's the relationship equivalent of wearing a helmet while biking—the road hazards are still there, but you're much better protected.

The Diversity Advantage: Different Support Types

Research also shows that diverse types of support contribute to relationship health in complementary ways:

- **Same-Gender Friendships**: Research by Dr. Geoffrey Greif found that maintaining strong same-gender friendships reduced inappropriate emotional dependency on romantic partners.

- **Cross-Gender Platonic Relationships**: Studies show that these friendships provide perspective on the opposite sex, which improves romantic communication when boundaries are clear.

- **Couple Friendships**: Research by Drs. Kathleen Holtz Deal and Victoria Hovey demonstrated that friendships with other couples provided relationship models and normalised challenges.

- **Family Connections**: Studies show that positive (but not enmeshed) family relationships provide historical context and continuity that strengthen romantic bonds.

- **Community Involvement**: Research reveals that couples participating in community activities report greater shared purpose and reduced focus on minor relationship irritations.

This research suggests that building different supportive connections creates a more robust foundation for romantic relationship health than focusing exclusively on one support source. It's the social equivalent of a diversified investment portfolio—much safer than putting all your emotional eggs in one basket.

Practical Application: Evidence-Based Support Building

Based on this research, consider these evidence-based approaches to building your support system:

1. **Diversify Support Types**: Develop different relationships for different support functions rather than relying on one or two people for everything.

2. **Maintain Friendship Continuity**: Research shows that longevity in friendships correlates with their protective effect on relationships. Invest in maintaining long-term connections.

3. **Create Couple-Individual Balance**: Research suggests maintaining a 60/40 balance between couple activities and individual social connections for optimal relationship health when you begin dating someone new.

4. **Establish Communication Channels**: Studies show that establishing communication protocols with

supporters before relationship challenges significantly improves their effectiveness.

5. **Address Network Conflicts**: Research indicates that tensions between romantic partners and social networks predict relationship problems. Proactively address these tensions rather than ignoring them.

Implementing these research-based approaches creates a support system that doesn't just feel good—it demonstrably improves one's chances of building and maintaining a healthy romantic relationship. Science for the relationship wins!

Case Studies: How Community Changes Dating Outcomes

To illustrate the transformative impact of support systems on dating patterns, let's examine how real people (with names and identifying details changed) have leveraged the community to change their relationship outcomes. There is no need to take notes—there won't be a quiz later.

Alex: From Isolation to Integration

Background: Alex, 34, had a pattern of becoming wholly absorbed in relationships, disconnecting from friends and focusing exclusively on his partners. When these inevitably intense relationships ended, he would find himself without support, leading to desperate attempts to reconcile or rushing into new relationships to fill the void. His friends had a nickname for his dating style: "The Romantic Black Hole."

Support System Development: During his dating sabbatical, Alex:

- Reconnected with three old friends, setting up a monthly dinner commitment

- Joined a recreational soccer league that met weekly

- Established a standing therapy appointment

- Created a "relationship council" of two friends and his sister who agreed to provide honest feedback about his dating patterns

Outcome: When Alex returned to dating, his new support system created dramatically different results:

- He maintained consistent friend connections even when strongly attracted to someone new

- His "council" helped him recognise when he was sliding into old absorption patterns

- The recreational league provided social connection regardless of his relationship status

- Regular therapy gave him a place to process relationship feelings without burdening new connections

"The difference was night and day," Alex reported. "When I met Jamie, I was attracted but didn't feel that desperate need to make her my entire world. I could enjoy developing our connection while maintaining all the other important parts of my life. Ironically, this more balanced approach created a healthier relationship than my previous all-in strategy ever did. Plus, Jamie actually likes that I have my friends and interests—it turns out suffocating someone with attention isn't as romantic as movies made it seem."

Sophia: The Reality Check Revolution

Background: Sophia, 29, had a pattern of ignoring relationship red flags, especially with charismatic but emotionally unavailable partners. She would rationalise concerning behaviours and dismiss friends' concerns, only to later realise they had seen problems she'd been blind to. She called her dating history "a museum of terrible decisions."

Support System Development: During her dating sabbatical, Sophia:

- Created a "reality check" group text with three trusted friends

- Committed to sharing detailed information about new dating connections rather than edited highlights

- Established a 24-hour reflection period before responding to concerning dating situations

- Developed a red flag inventory based on past relationships

- Joined a relationship skills group led by a therapist

Outcome: When Sophia resumed dating, her support system dramatically improved her pattern recognition:

- She began consulting her reality check group when unsure about dating situations

- The 24-hour reflection period prevented impulsive decisions based on chemistry alone

- Her red flag inventory, reviewed regularly with her support group, kept warning signs visible

- The skills group provided ongoing education about healthy versus unhealthy dynamics

"I was on a third date with someone who seemed perfect on paper," Sophia shared. "When he commented on 'training' his ex to behave differently, I would have ignored it. Instead, I shared it with my reality check group. Their responses helped me see this wasn't just a poor word choice but a control pattern similar to what I'd experienced before. I ended things early instead of discovering this month into another painful relationship. My friends saved me from dating another guy who thought women were Pokémon to be trained!"

Marcus: The Mentor Transformation

Background: Marcus, 42, grew up without positive relationship models. His parents' marriage was conflictual, and his community emphasised enduring unhappy relationships rather than creating healthy ones. Without positive examples, Marcus had no template for a healthy partnership in practice. His idea of relationships came primarily from 90s sitcoms—not exactly a recipe for success.

Support System Development: During his dating sabbatical, Marcus:

- Identified three couples whose relationships he admired

- Asked if they would be willing to share insights about their relationship journeys

- Created a monthly "relationship wisdom dinner" where he invited these mentors

- Joined a men's group focused on emotional intelligence and relationship skills

- Began volunteering at a community centre where he interacted with diverse families

Outcome: This mentoring approach transformed Marcus's understanding of relationships:

- He gained concrete examples of how healthy conflicts could be navigated

- He learned that good relationships required ongoing intention, not just finding "the right person."

- He developed a more realistic view of everyday relationship challenges

- He absorbed relationship skills through observation that no book could have taught him

"Before my mentors, I thought relationships were either perfect or failing," Marcus explained. "Seeing couples talk openly about their challenges completely changed my perspective. When I started dating Rachel, I approached our first disagreement differently. Instead of seeing it as a sign we weren't meant to be, I saw it as an opportunity to develop our communication like my mentors did. I finally got the relationship instruction manual I never received growing up."

Elena: The Reciprocal Support Network

Background: Elena, 37, struggled with feeling burdensome when asking for emotional support. She would provide extensive support to friends but rarely reached out when she needed help, leading to lopsided relationships and eventual burnout. This pattern extended to dating, where she would prioritise her partner's needs while minimising her own. She was essentially everyone's emotional support human with no support of her own.

Support System Development: During her dating sabbatical, Elena:

- joined a women's circle that met biweekly with an explicit focus on mutual support

- Created a "support exchange" with two friends where each person took turns being supported

- Worked with a therapist on her discomfort with receiving versus giving

- Developed clear language for asking for different types of support

- Practiced small support requests to build her "receiving muscle."

Outcome: This reciprocal support approach created transformative change in Elena's dating patterns:

- She entered new dating situations with experience articulating her needs

- She could recognise when she was slipping into caretaker mode at the expense of her needs

- She had evidence that relationships could be balanced rather than one-sided

- She brought the expectation of reciprocity rather than self-sacrifice to new connections

"My support network gave me practice in asking for help and receiving it gracefully," Elena shared. "This completely changed my dating approach. With Daniel, I was able to express my needs from the beginning rather than pretending I was fine with whatever he wanted. The amazing thing was that he appreciated my clarity—it created safety for him, too. Turns out mind-reading isn't a prerequisite for a good relationship. Who knew?"

Common Themes Across Case Studies

While each person's journey was unique, several common themes emerged across these support system transformations:

1. **Diversity of Support**: Those who created multi-person, multi-function support networks showed greater resilience than those relying on one or two primary supporters.

2. **Specificity of Function**: The most effective support systems clearly define different roles rather than expecting all supporters to serve all functions.

3. **Reciprocal Design**: Sustainable support systems allow people to contribute value to their supporters rather than only receiving.

4. **Proactive Engagement**: Those who established regular support connections before crises arose reported better outcomes than those who reached out only when problems developed.

5. **Continuous Evolution**: Effective support systems were periodically evaluated and adjusted as needs and circumstances changed.

These themes suggest that building an effective support system isn't about finding perfect people but creating intentional connections with explicit functions, regular engagement, and mutual benefit. It's less like finding a unicorn and more like assembling your own personal Avengers team—each with different powers but working toward a common goal.

Practical Tool: The Support System Design Workshop

To apply the principles in this chapter, this workshop helps you design a comprehensive support system for your dating journey. Set aside 2-3 hours for this transformative exercise. Yes, I know that's a big time commitment, but so is sobbing over another heartbreak while your cat judges you from across the room.

Materials Needed:

- Several sheets of paper
- Coloured markers or pens
- Post-it notes or small papers

- Your journal from previous Dating Detox exercises
- Snacks (not technically required but highly recommended)

Step 1: Support Function Identification (30 mins)

List all the different support functions you need for healthy dating, such as:

- Pattern recognition assistance
- Emotional processing space
- Honest feedback on potential partners
- Healthy relationship modelling
- Meaningful connection outside of dating
- Professional guidance on specific issues
- Celebration of progress and growth

For each function, note:

- How frequently do you need this support
- What specific form would be most helpful
- What makes someone well-suited to provide this function

Step 2: Potential Supporter Inventory (30 mins)

Create a comprehensive list of people who might be part of your support system:

- Current close friends
- Family members with healthy relationship perspectives
- Former connections who could be rekindled
- New acquaintances with the potential for a deeper connection
- Professional resources (therapists, coaches, groups)
- Communities where you might find additional supporters

For each potential supporter, note:

- Their strengths and areas of wisdom
- Their availability and communication preferences
- The history and quality of your connection
- Their relationship health and perspective

Step 3: Connection Mapping (30 mins)

Create a visual map of your ideal support system:

1. Draw yourself in the centre of a page

2. Create different "spokes" representing the support functions you identified

3. Place potential supporters along these spokes based on their suitability

4. Use different colours to indicate:

    - Current active connections

    - Connections needing strengthening

    - New connections to develop

This visual map helps you identify your current network's strengths and areas for development. Plus, with all those markers, you can channel your inner kindergartner.

Step 4: Support Activation Planning (30 mins)

For each person you want to include in your support system, create an activation plan:

For Existing Connections:

- How will you communicate your desire for this specific support?

- What clear requests will make it easy for them to help effectively?

- How will you create reciprocity in the relationship?

- What boundaries need to be established for this support to work?

For New Connections:

- What specific steps will initiate this connection?

- How will you gradually build the trust needed for support?

- What value can you offer in the relationship?

- What milestones will indicate readiness for more substantial support?

Step 5: Support Protocol Development (30 mins)

Create specific protocols for engaging your support system:

Regular Connection Protocols:

- Schedule regular check-ins with key supporters

- Create topics or questions for these scheduled connections

- Develop reminders and accountability for maintaining these touchpoints

Situation-Specific Protocols:

- For dating red flags: Who to contact and how

- For chemistry confusion: What support should be activated and when

- For post-date processing: Your reflection and sharing process

- For relationship decisions: Your consultation approach

Appreciation Practices:

- How you'll express gratitude to your supporters

- Ways you'll track the impact of their support

- Methods for celebrating their contribution to your growth

Step 6: Implementation Timeline (30 mins)

Create a week-by-week plan for building your support system:

- Week 1: Initial conversations with 2-3 core supporters

- Week 2: Schedule and hold the first structured check-ins

- Week 3: Reach out to one new potential connection

- Week 4: Review and adjust based on initial experiences

Continue mapping specific actions through the first two months to ensure your support system moves from concept to reality. Otherwise, this whole exercise becomes as useful as that gym membership you bought in January and forgot about by February.

Workshop Completion: The Support Commitment

Conclude the workshop by writing a commitment to yourself about building and maintaining your support system. Sign and date this commitment as a reminder of its importance to your dating success.

Rachel found this workshop transformative: "I realised I had been approaching support all wrong—either trying to do everything alone or dumping all my needs on one friend. Creating a diversified support system with specific functions completely changed my approach. Now, I have different people with different needs, and I'm also clear about how I support them in return. My dating life feels completely different with this foundation beneath it. I'm no longer one relationship problem away from a complete emotional breakdown, which it turns out is pretty attractive!"

As you conclude this chapter and continue your dating sabbatical, remember that building a strong support system isn't self-indulgent or weak—it's one of the most practical steps to creating a healthy romantic relationship.

You create the conditions where healthy love can flourish by intentionally developing connections that provide accountability, perspective, modelling, and emotional support. Your willingness to build this foundation demonstrates the relationship skills that make you a valuable partner: communication, reciprocity, self-awareness, and community building.

And hey, even if you're still figuring out the whole dating thing, you'll have awesome people to hang out with. That's what I call a win-win!

CHAPTER 8:

Strategic Dating

From Dating Disaster to Dating Mastermind

Woohoo! You've reached Part III of your dating transformation journey! If you've completed your dating detox and invested in building your relationship with yourself, give yourself a massive high-five. You've already tackled the tough stuff. Now comes the part that might feel more familiar—dating again—but trust me, we're doing it differently this time.

Intentional vs. Passive Partner Finding: Choose Your Adventure

Let's start with a hard truth: most of us approach dating like we're waiting for lightning to strike—while standing in a basement. We:

- Hope to "magically bump into" our soulmate at the grocery store (probably while wearing our rattiest sweatpants)

- Wait for that mythical "perfect timing" (spoiler: it doesn't exist)

- Let apps dictate our love lives while we swipe mindlessly during commercials

- Date whoever shows interest (because hey, they picked me!)

- Follow the "chemistry compass" even when it leads us straight into relationship quicksand

- Slide into relationships based on momentum rather than compatibility (oops, I've been sleeping over for six months; guess we're serious now?)

This passive approach essentially treats love like a lottery ticket—and let's be honest, when was the last time you won more than $5 in a lottery?

Strategic dating flips the script. It recognises that finding a compatible partner is an internal and external process that benefits from thoughtful intention rather than passive hoping. It's like the difference between "hoping" to get in shape and joining a gym with a workout plan.

The Mindset Shift: From Hopeful Romantic to Love Strategist

When Marcus returned to dating after his sabbatical, he noticed an immediate difference: "Before, I was basically throwing myself into the dating pool and hoping someone great would swim by. Now I feel like I'm navigating with a map and compass—I know what I'm looking for and have a plan for finding it."

This shift doesn't mean becoming some cold, calculating romance robot. It means:

1. Dating with clarity about your values and relationship vision instead of playing romantic roulette

2. Making conscious choices about where and how you meet potential partners rather than defaulting to wherever's convenient (goodbye, 2 AM bar connections!)

3. Evaluating compatibility systematically rather than being led solely by the "OMG they're hot" factor

4. Progressing relationships intentionally rather than waking up one-day thinking, "Wait, how did I get here?"

5. Maintaining your growth and boundaries throughout the dating process (revolutionary concept, I know)

As Aisha put it: "Before my sabbatical, I was essentially auditioning for roles in other people's lives—trying to be whatever would make them choose me. I'm interviewing potential co-creators for the relationship I want to build. The power dynamic is completely different."

The Four Components of Strategic Dating (No MBA Required)

Strategic dating consists of four interconnected elements:

1. **Strategic Selection**: Deliberately choosing dating contexts and methods that maximise your chances of meeting compatible partners (instead of hoping your soulmate also shops at Target on Tuesday evenings)

2. **Strategic Pacing**: Consciously managing the progression of connections rather than defaulting to either avoidance ("let's text for 6 months before meeting") or premature merging ("I've cleared a drawer for you after our third date")

3. **Strategic Evaluation**: Systematically assessing compatibility based on your relationship vision rather than chemistry alone (because chemistry got you into trouble the last three times, remember?)

4. **Strategic Balance**: Maintaining equilibrium between dating activity and the rest of your life rather than falling into the all-or-nothing trap of "I'm either dating 24/7 or sworn off love forever."

Online and Offline Dating Strategies: A Foot in Both Worlds

The question isn't whether to date online or offline—it's how to strategically use both channels without losing your sanity.

The Strategic Approach to Dating Apps (Without Becoming a Swipe Zombie)

Dating apps get plenty of well-deserved eye-rolls. They can turn humans into shopping items, foster connections shallower than a kiddie pool, and overwhelm you with more options than a cereal aisle. However, when used strategically, they're powerful tools for expanding your dating pool beyond your immediate circle of friends and that one cute barista.

Strategic App Selection:

Not all dating apps are created equal. Different platforms attract different crowds. Instead of defaulting to whatever app your friend mentioned last week, strategically selected based on the following:

1. **Relationship intention alignment**: Some apps attract users primarily seeking serious relationships (e.g., Match, Hinge), while others skew toward "let's see where this goes...probably nowhere" connections (looking at you, Tinder).

2. **Demographic alignment**: Different apps attract different age ranges, educational backgrounds, and interest groups. Choose accordingly unless you're specifically looking for an age-gap relationship or someone with a radically different background.

3. **Interaction method**: Some apps give users more control over who can contact them, reducing the chances you'll be overwhelmed with messages from people whose opening line is "hey."

4. **Profile depth**: Platforms vary in how much substantive information they encourage. If you can't express anything beyond your height and a beach photo, maybe look elsewhere.

Mia tested multiple apps before settling on two aligned with her goals: "I chose one app known for relationship-minded users, and another focused on my specific interest community. This targeted approach resulted in fewer but higher-quality matches than when I was on five general apps just playing dating app bingo."

Strategic Profile Creation:

Your dating profile isn't just an advertisement—it's a filtering tool. Its purpose is to attract compatible people while helping incompatible ones self-select out. Strategic profiles:

1. Lead with values rather than just activities or superficial traits ("I value deep conversations and personal growth" vs "I like hiking and pizza")

2. Include "polarising" elements that will attract your people and repel others (if your dark humour is essential to who you are, show it—the right people will laugh)

3. Use specific examples rather than generic descriptions ("I spend Sunday mornings reading with my coffee on the porch" vs. "I enjoy relaxing")

4. Showcase authentic aspects of yourself rather than what you think is most marketable (your Dungeons & Dragons obsession might be precisely what your future partner is searching for)

5. Include conversation hooks that make it easy for compatible people to engage (give them something specific to respond to besides your appearance)

Jason transformed his generic profile ("I enjoy hiking, good food, and travelling") into one that revealed his actual personality and values ("Looking for someone who appreciates deep conversations about philosophy, isn't afraid of my horrible puns, and values growth over perfection"). "I get fewer matches now," he noted, "but the conversations instantly go deeper and more often lead to meaningful connections rather than 'what's up?' exchanges that die after three messages."

Strategic Swiping and Selection:

The default app behaviour of rapid-fire swiping based on photos creates a neurochemical hit without leading to quality connections. It's the dating equivalent of empty calories. Strategic selection involves:

1. Time-bounded swiping sessions rather than endless scrolling until your thumb cramps

2. Thorough profile review before swiping right (yes, actually read what they wrote)

3. Explicit compatibility assessment based on your relationship vision (not just "they're cute")

4. Limiting active conversations to ensure quality engagement (nobody needs 18 half-hearted chats going at once)

5. Regular app breaks to prevent burnout and those moments when you start to think, "Are all humans terrible?"

Elena implemented a "three-message rule," where she would exchange at least three substantial messages before agreeing to meet someone. "This simple boundary filtered out people who weren't willing to invest minimal effort in conversation, saving me countless wasted dates with people who were just collecting dinner companions."

The Strategic Approach to Offline Meetings (Yes, People Still Meet in Real Life)

While apps provide volume, meeting potential partners offline often creates higher-quality initial connections. Offline meetings benefit from contextual information, immediate physical presence and energy assessment, and shared experiences as the foundation for conversations beyond "So...what do you do?"

Strategic Context Selection:

Not all offline meeting contexts are equally promising. Strategic context selection involves:

1. **Alignment with your values and interests** so you meet people who share them (volunteer for that environmental cause if sustainability matters to you)

2. **Recurring rather than one-time events** that allow connections to develop naturally (a weekly class beats a one-off workshop)

3. **Interaction-friendly environments** that facilitate conversation (good luck having a meaningful exchange at a concert where you can't hear yourself think)

4. **Gender balance** appropriate to your dating goals (if you're looking for men, that 90% female yoga class might not be your strategic best bet)

5. **New contexts** that expand your social circle rather than recycling the same pools (if you've already dated everyone at your workplace, maybe branch out)

Passionate about social justice, Tomas began volunteering regularly with a community organisation aligned with his values. "Instead of hoping to meet someone who says they care about the same things, I'm meeting people who show up to do the work. We already share values and experiences to build upon—even if we don't end up dating, I've made meaningful connections."

Strategic Social Network Activation:

Your existing social connections are potent resources for meeting compatible partners, but most people underutilise them. Strategic approaches include:

1. **Explicitly communicating your dating intentions** to friends and trusted connections (they can't help if they don't know you're looking)

2. **Providing specific compatibility indicators** rather than vague requests ("I value intellectual curiosity and emotional openness" beats "Set me up with someone nice")

3. **Creating low-pressure group gatherings** that allow natural interaction with potential introductions (much better than the awkward blind date setup)

4. **Following up on promising connections** rather than waiting for the magic to happen ("I enjoyed meeting your friend Jamie; would you mind if I asked for their number?")

5. **Expressing genuine appreciation** for introductions regardless of outcome (your friends aren't professional matchmakers, but they are trying to help)

Sarah created what she called "connection dinners," where she invited a mix of established friends and new acquaintances with potential compatibility. "It removed the awkwardness of blind dates while creating natural opportunities to interact with people my friends thought I might click with. Plus, I often make new friends even with no romantic spark—it's a win-win."

Strategic Social Skills Development:

Meeting people offline requires social skills many have neglected in the digital age. Let's be honest—some of us have forgotten how to start a conversation without the cushion of a text delay. Strategic development involves:

1. **Practicing approachability signals** like open body language and genuine smiles (not the frozen grimace of social anxiety)

2. **Developing organic conversation starters** appropriate to different contexts (commenting on shared experiences rather than defaulting to weather talk)

3. **Cultivating genuine curiosity** about others rather than self-presentation (people sense when you're actually interested vs. waiting for your turn to talk)

4. **Build comfort by expressing interest** directly but respectfully (the lost art of "I've enjoyed talking with you. Would you like to get coffee sometime?")

5. **Normalizing rejection as information** rather than judgment (not everyone will be interested, and that's helpful information)

After relying exclusively on apps for years, Carlos worked with a social coach to develop his in-person skills. "I realised I needed to relearn how to start conversations that flowed naturally into potential connection. The coach helped me practice in low-stakes environments until it felt more comfortable. Now I can approach someone at a bookstore without feeling like I'm having a heart attack."

Integration: Creating Your Channel Strategy (Without Going Insane)

The most effective approach combines online and offline channels in a strategic balance that plays to the strengths of each while mitigating the drawbacks.

The Channel Balance Assessment:

Evaluate your current approach by asking:

1. Am I overly dependent on a single channel? (If your phone died, would your dating life cease to exist?)

2. Which channel has historically led to my most compatible connections? (Data doesn't lie)

3. Which channel creates the most dating fatigue or leaves me feeling like I want to join a monastery?

4. How does each channel align with my current lifestyle and availability? (Be realistic here)

5. Which channel gives me the most accurate information about potential compatibility? (Think about your past dating disasters)

The Integrated Channel Strategy:

Based on your assessment, create a customised approach that might include:

- Using apps during specific time-bounded sessions rather than constant availability (dating apps are not meant to be your digital pacifier)

- Scheduling regular participation in value-aligned in-person communities (where people already share at least one important value with you)

- Creating a rhythm of online and offline dating rather than consuming all your energy in one channel (diversification isn't just for financial portfolios)

- Adjusting your strategy seasonally based on life circumstances and results (flexibility prevents burnout)

Maya created a balanced approach: "I check dating apps on Sunday and Wednesday evenings only, for no more than 30 minutes. I participate in my hiking group and volunteer organization weekly and have dinner with different friend groups monthly. This creates a steady stream of new connections without dating taking over my life. I'm no longer that friend who's either completely absorbed in a new dating app or swearing off relationships forever."

The Quality Over Quantity Approach (Stop Dating Like You're Sampling Free Cheese at Costco)

Perhaps the most transformative shift in strategic dating is moving from a volume-based to a quality-based approach. The conventional wisdom that dating is a "numbers game" has led many people to prioritise the quantity of dates over the quality of connections—with diminishing returns and an ever-growing collection of bad date stories.

The Problem with Dating Volume

Research in decision psychology reveals that excessive options decrease satisfaction with choices and increase decision fatigue. The "paradox of choice" is particularly relevant to dating, where app culture has created unprecedented volumes of potential connections.

The volume approach creates several problems:

1. **Decision fatigue** leads to poor partner selection judgments (by date #5 in a week, everyone starts to blur together)

2. **Comparison overload** makes it difficult to assess compatibility properly ("Wait, was this the one who liked hiking or was that yesterday's date?")

3. **Disposability mindset** decreases investment in promising connections (why work through minor issues when 50 new matches are waiting?)

4. **Emotional burnout** reduces authentic presence with potential partners (it's hard to be genuine when you're exhausted)

5. **Time diffusion** spreads your energy too thinly for meaningful connection (dating becomes another task to be completed rather than an opportunity for connection)

Jason described his volume-dating burnout: "I was going on three to four first dates every week, essentially turning dating into a part-time job. By the fourth date each week, I couldn't remember what I'd already told the person across from me. No one was getting the real me because I was too exhausted to be present. I was a dating zombie, going through the motions."

The Strategic Alternative: Qualified Leads (Dating Like a Pro, Not a Desperate Rookie)

Rather than maximising date volume, strategic dating focuses on increasing the quality of your dating "leads"—the potential partners you choose to invest time in meeting and getting to know.

This approach borrows from business principles, where qualified leads (prospects with a higher alignment probability) receive focused attention rather than resources being spread across all possible contacts. Think of it as having a few meaningful conversations at a party versus trying to chat briefly with everyone in the room.

Principles of the Qualified Lead Approach:

1. **Pre-qualification**: Invest more time in assessment before meeting in person (this isn't an interrogation, but basic compatibility checking saves everyone time)

2. **Progressive engagement**: Increase investment as compatibility indicators strengthen (don't plan your wedding after one good date)

3. **Concurrent limitation**: Engage with only as many connections as you can authentically attend to (for most humans, this isn't 12)

4. **Intentional pacing**: Allow connections to develop rhythm rather than forcing acceleration (or stalling indefinitely)

5. **Full presence**: Give each interaction your authentic attention rather than hedging across multiple options (put the phone down when you're on a date)

Sophia shifted to this approach after her dating sabbatical: "Instead of the constant swiping and first-date hamster wheel, I now spend more time in the selection and early conversation phase. I might only go on one date every couple of weeks, but the connection quality is dramatically higher, and I'm enjoying the process instead of dreading it. Dating feels like an adventure again rather than a second job."

Implementing the Quality Approach: Practical Strategies

The Pre-Date Qualification Process:

Develop a personalised process for assessing potential compatibility before investing in in-person meetings:

1. **Value alignment scanning**: Look for indicators of compatibility with your core values (if family is important to you, does this person mention theirs?)

2. **Communication quality assessment**: Evaluate depth, reciprocity, and authenticity of early exchanges (are they asking thoughtful questions or just responding with "haha cool"?)

3. **Red flag screening**: Check for the presence of your established red flags (we all have them, and they're usually there for good reason)

4. **Intention clarification**: Ensure mutual understanding of relationship goals (if you want a long-term relationship and they want "nothing serious," believe them)

5. **Energy examination**: Notice how interactions affect your energy levels (do you feel drained or energised after communicating?)

This process isn't about creating rigid checklists but about consciously evaluating alignment before investing significant time and emotional energy. It's the difference between throwing darts blindfolded and actually aiming at the target.

The Investment Ladder:

Instead of the conventional rushing or stalling patterns, create a progressive investment approach:

1. **Initial exchanges**: Brief, focused on essential compatibility (not drawn-out texting marathons)

2. **Expanded conversation**: Deeper exploration of values and experiences (beyond favourite Netflix shows)

3. **First meeting**: Brief, low-pressure context focused on real-life chemistry (coffee beats a five-course dinner for first encounters)

4. **Subsequent dates**: Progressive increase in time investment and vulnerability (as comfort and interest grow)

5. **Exclusivity consideration**: Intentional evaluation rather than default sliding (a conscious choice, not "I guess we're exclusive now?")

This gradual approach allows incompatibilities to surface before excessive emotional investment while giving promising connections space to develop authentically. Think of it as progressive weight training rather than trying to deadlift 300 pounds on day one.

The Simultaneous Connection Limit:

Determine how many potential connections you can authentically engage with based on:

1. Your current life commitments and available time (be realistic)

2. Your emotional bandwidth for new connections (also be realistic)

3. Your ability to remain present and avoid comparison (comparing potential partners is the fastest way to dating confusion)

4. Your clarity in differentiating between connections (if they all blur together, you're juggling too many)

For many people, this limit is 2-3 potential connections in the early stages, decreasing to 1 as a relationship progresses toward exclusivity. Remember, you're looking for quality over quantity.

Carlos implemented a strict two-person limit: "When I reach my conversation limit, I pause swiping and new conversations until one naturally concludes or progresses. This keeps me from treating people as disposable options and helps me give each connection a fair evaluation. I'm no longer that person with 15 half-hearted text exchanges going at once."

Quality Metrics: Beyond Chemistry and Convenience

The quality approach requires moving beyond the default physical attraction and logistical convenience metrics to more substantive evaluation criteria. Yes, chemistry matters—but it's not the only thing that matters.

Alternative Quality Metrics:

1. **Conversational depth**: The level of meaningful exchange beyond small talk (can you discuss things that matter?)

2. **Value resonance**: The degree of alignment on core principles that matter to you (not whether you both like the same movies)

3. **Emotional impact**: How interactions affect your emotional state and energy (do you feel better or worse after spending time with them?)

4. **Growth potential**: The capacity for mutual development and support (can you both improve together?)

5. **Ease factor**: The natural flow of interaction without forced compatibility (relationships shouldn't feel like pushing a boulder uphill)

Tanya developed a post-date reflection practice using these metrics: "After each date, I journal about these five factors rather than just general impressions or chemistry. It helps me see patterns I might miss in the moment and makes evaluation more about compatibility than fleeting feelings. I'm no longer making decisions based solely on 'butterflies' or 'spark'—which, let's be honest, haven't led me to great relationships in the past."

Your Personal Dating Plan: From Chaos to Strategy

To implement strategic dating effectively, you need a personalised plan that reflects your unique values, circumstances, and relationship goals. The accompanying workbook contains a comprehensive exercise to create that plan. For now, consider these key questions:

- Which meeting methods have historically connected you with compatible people?

- What patterns emerge in your dating history that you want to change?

- How much time, emotional energy, and financial resources can you realistically dedicate to dating?

- What are your strengths and growth areas in the dating process?

- How will you balance online and offline approaches?

- What system will you use to assess compatibility efficiently?

- How will you maintain boundaries and well-being throughout the process?

Maya described her experience with this planning process: "Creating a detailed dating plan felt strange at first—almost too structured for something as emotional as dating. But having this framework has been incredibly liberating. I'm no longer reacting to whatever dating situation comes my way; I'm actively creating the conditions for meaningful connection while protecting my energy and boundaries. For the first time, I feel in control of my dating life rather than at the mercy of it."

The Research Shows: Dating Smarter Works

Relationship science confirms that strategic dating isn't just theory—it produces better results. Studies consistently show that:

- Meeting contexts that align with personal values increases compatibility

- Moderate progression pacing (neither too rushed nor too hesitant) correlates with relationship satisfaction

- Multiple information sources improve partner selection accuracy

- Excessive dating options decrease satisfaction with chosen partners

Dr Elena Greenberg, a relationship researcher, summarises: "The data consistently shows that intentional, value-aligned meeting contexts combined with thoughtful progression significantly outperform the 'maximising options' approach that dominates modern dating culture. Quality-focused strategies produce better outcomes than volume-based approaches. In other words, dating fewer people more intentionally works better than dating countless people haphazardly."

The Dating Efficiency Matrix: Work Smarter, Not Harder

While dating shouldn't be reduced to pure efficiency (we're not optimising a supply chain here), most of us have limited time and emotional energy. The Dating Efficiency Matrix helps you evaluate potential dating activities based on:

- **Compatibility Yield**: How likely an activity is to connect you with compatible partners

- **Resource Investment**: The combined time, emotional, and financial resources required

Creating your personal matrix helps identify:

- **Efficiency Stars**: High-yield, low-investment activities to prioritise

- **Strategic Investments**: High-yield activities worth significant investment

- **Occasional Opportunities**: Low-yield, low-investment activities for occasional engagement

- **Efficiency Drains**: Low-yield, high-investment activities to eliminate

As Elena discovered: "I realised I was investing tremendous energy in activities with terrible return rates while underutilising my most efficient channels. By redirecting just 25% of my dating energy to higher-yield activities, I doubled the number of compatible connections and enjoyed the process more. I stopped treating dating like a part-time job with terrible pay."

Balancing Efficiency and Serendipity: Leave Room for Magic

While efficiency is essential, maintaining space for unexpected connections keeps dating joyful. Strategic dating isn't about eliminating all spontaneity—it's about being intentional about where you invest most of your dating resources while leaving room for surprise.

The key is to:

- Reserve 10-20% of your dating energy for "serendipity activities" without specific expectations

- Remain open to unexpected connections in everyday contexts

- Create conditions for "engineered serendipity" in aligned contexts

Carlos effectively maintained this balance: "I approach dating systematically about 80% of the time, focusing on high-efficiency methods. However, I also leave room for unexpected connections. The difference is that I'm no longer relying on luck as my primary strategy—I'm creating the conditions for compatible connections while remaining open to surprise. It's the difference between hoping to win the lottery and making smart investments while buying an occasional lottery ticket for fun."

As you implement strategic dating, remember that the goal isn't to turn romance into a spreadsheet exercise. It's to bring intention and awareness to a process that too often defaults to passivity and reaction.

By approaching dating strategically, you honour yourself and your potential partners by creating conditions where genuine connection can flourish without unnecessary confusion or wasted effort. You're not manipulating outcomes but aligning your actions with your intentions.

The next chapter will explore how to build authentic connection skills that deepen these strategically initiated relationships into meaningful bonds. Finding your person is just the beginning—building something beautiful together is where the real adventure starts.

CHAPTER 9:

Authentic Connection Skills - The Art of Not Being Awkward

The Science of Deep Bonding (Without the Lab Coat)

Alright, you've done your homework—sort out your inner baggage, create that vision board for your dream relationship, and approach dating with actual strategy instead of just hoping for the best. High five for that! Now comes the trickiest skill of all: connecting with another human being without making both of you want to fake an emergency phone call.

It sounds straightforward, right? We're supposedly social creatures hardwired to connect. Yet, genuine connection has become as rare as a phone battery that lasts all day. Many of us are stuck in an endless loop of the same surface-level conversations, wondering why dating feels emptier than our bank accounts after rent day—despite meeting plenty of perfectly nice people who love travel, tacos, and The Office.

Here's the thing nobody tells you: genuine connection is both an art and a science, with specific ingredients that you can actually understand and develop. It's not just about finding someone hot who also likes your favourite band—it's about creating a special quality of interaction that builds safety, understanding, and genuine intimacy.

The Connection Paradox (Or Why This Stuff Is So Confusing)

This fascinating paradox is at the heart of real connection: it requires courage, safety, vulnerability, boundaries, spontaneity, AND intention. No wonder it feels simultaneously super simple and maddeningly tricky!

As relationship researcher Dr Barbara Fredrickson explains (in what I imagine is her TED Talk voice): "Love and connection don't just happen to you—they're biological processes that you can actively participate in creating." Her research shows that connection isn't just an emotional state where you get butterflies—it's actually a biological synchronisation between two nervous systems that you can deliberately cultivate.

This shifts our whole perspective from passively hoping to experience a connection to actively creating it together. It's less about finding that mythical "perfect person" and more about developing the ability to connect authentically with compatible humans.

The Three Levels of Connection (Because Everything Needs Levels)

Research in interpersonal neurobiology identifies three distinct levels of connection, each building on the previous:

Level 1: Basic Resonance - The "You Exist!" Level

This is the fundamental sense of being seen and acknowledged by another person. Neuroscientist Stephen Porges calls it the "perception of safety," which sounds much fancier than "this person doesn't make me want to run away." This initial level involves:

- paying attention to each other (revolutionary, I know)
- Responding to basic social cues instead of staring at your phone
- The sense that the other person registers your existence as a fellow human and not just a potential dating inventory

Level 2: Emotional Atonement - The "You Get Me!" Level

This is where you feel understood and cared for in your emotional reality—not just acknowledged as a talking being. This mid-level connection includes:

- Recognition of emotional states beyond "fine" and "good"
- Appropriate response to emotional signals (not just "That's crazy!")
- The sense of being emotionally "gotten" without having to explain yourself fifteen times
- Mutual empathy that doesn't require an instruction manual

Level 3: Deep Synchrony - The "We're in This Together" Level

This is the profound state where two people experience a sense of "we" without losing their identities (no creepy mind-melding required). This advanced connection involves:

- Physiological synchronisation (heart rate, breathing patterns) that happens naturally, not because you're both doing a guided meditation

- Creating meaning together, not just agreeing on Netflix shows

- Influencing each other's growth in ways that don't involve nagging

- The ability to move between independence and togetherness without getting clingy or distant

Most dating interactions never progress beyond superficial resonance—polite exchanges that acknowledge each other's physical presence but create all the genuine connection of ordering coffee from a barista. Developing skills to navigate all three levels transforms your capacity for authentic relationships.

Why Connection Skills Matter More Than Ever (Blame the Apps)

In previous generations, people often connected through shared circumstances, community integration, and limited options. When only three eligible people were in your village, you figured out how to connect with at least one! Modern dating, however, has eliminated many of these structural supports, replacing them with:

- Abundant but superficial choice (like a buffet where everything tastes slightly bland)

- Text-based communication that removes all helpful nonverbal cues (good luck deciphering "k")

- Entertainment-oriented dating that prioritises activities over actual human interaction

- Efficiency-focused encounters that treat connection development like an Amazon delivery

This context makes deliberate connection skills more essential than ever. As Dr. John Gottman notes, "In today's relationship landscape, the ability to create authentic connection has moved from an intuitive process to a skill set that often requires conscious development." In other words, what used to happen naturally now requires some intentional effort—kind of like how we once didn't need to worry about screen time, but here we are.

Let's explore how to develop these skills across three key domains of authentic connection!

Vulnerability Without Oversharing (Or: How Not to Trauma Dump on Date One)

Vulnerability has become such a relationship buzzword that you'd think sharing your deepest insecurities over appetisers was the way to go. But actual vulnerability isn't about emotional dumping, trauma sharing, or premature intimacy—it's about showing up authentically despite the risk of rejection.

The Vulnerability Spectrum

Vulnerability exists on a spectrum from inauthentically closed to open inappropriately:

Inauthentically Closed:

- Presenting only your Instagram-worthy aspects

- Hiding genuine thoughts, feelings, and experiences like they're state secrets

- Avoiding topics that might reveal your true self

- Maintaining a facade of perfection that would exhaust a Broadway performer

Appropriately Vulnerable:

- Gradually revealing authentic aspects of yourself (like peeling an onion, but less crying)

- Sharing thoughts, feelings, and experiences relevant to the relationship stage

- Taking emotional risks at a pace that allows safety to develop

- Allowing the real you to be seen, imperfections and all

Inappropriately Open:

- Sharing your entire therapy journey before the server brings water

- Using disclosure as a shortcut to intimacy

- Emotional dumping without regard for the poor person sitting across from you

- Sharing without appropriate boundaries or context

Most of us ping-pong between being too closed and occasionally overcorrecting with inappropriate openness (especially after that second glass of wine). The skill lies in finding the middle path of appropriate vulnerability that builds connection without making the other person want to fake a family emergency.

Research by Dr Arthur Aron found that gradual, reciprocal vulnerability—where disclosure deepens progressively and is matched by the other person—creates the most substantial bonding effect. This "vulnerability dance" builds trust through mutual risk-taking that respects the relationship's development stage.

The Four Components of Healthy Vulnerability

Effective vulnerability in dating involves four essential elements:

1. Authenticity:

Sharing your thoughts, feelings, and experiences rather than what you think the other person wants to hear. This includes:

- Expressing your real opinions even when they might differ ("Actually, I thought that movie was pretty terrible...")

- Naming your true feelings rather than presenting what seems most appealing

- Being honest about your life circumstances and history (within appropriate boundaries)

2. Relevance:

Ensuring your vulnerable sharing is appropriate to where you are in the relationship. This involves:

- Matching disclosure depth to the established trust level (childhood trauma? Date twelve. Bad day at work? Date two.)

- Sharing information that helps the other person understand you better

- Focusing on experiences and feelings relevant to your current interaction

3. Reciprocity:

Creating a balanced exchange where vulnerability flows in both directions. This includes:

- Noticing whether the other person matches your disclosure level or changes the subject faster than a politician dodging questions

- Responding appropriately to their vulnerability with understanding

- Avoiding one-sided sharing that creates imbalance

4. Boundary Awareness:

Maintaining healthy limits, even in vulnerability. This involves:

- Distinguishing between productive vulnerability and trauma dumping

- Respecting your privacy needs around specific topics

- Checking in with yourself about comfort levels during sharing

Jason struggled with appropriate vulnerability after years of presenting only his most polished self on dates. "I went from showing only my highlights reel to occasionally sharing way too much too soon," he explained. "Learning the middle path of authentic but appropriately paced vulnerability completely changed my dating experience. For the first time, I felt like the real me was connecting with the real them, not just our carefully curated personas trying to impress each other."

Practical Vulnerability Techniques

Here are some specific practices you can implement to develop appropriate vulnerability:

The Personal Share Progression:

Practice gradually deepening self-disclosure through these levels:

1. Observable facts about yourself (interests, activities, general background)

2. Thoughts and perspectives on external topics (views on issues, ideas, concepts)

3. Personal preferences and mild emotions (likes, dislikes, hopes, simple joys)

4. Deeper values and meaningful experiences (what matters to you and why)

5. Insecurities, fears, and profound emotions (when appropriate trust exists)

This progression creates a natural vulnerability development that builds connections without making the other person feel like they accidentally signed up for an intensive therapy workshop.

The Authenticity Check-In:

Before and during dates, briefly check in with yourself:

- Am I presenting a curated version of myself or my authentic self?

- What am I hiding that might create a connection if shared more openly?

- Am I saying what I think/feel or what I think they want to hear?

This simple practice increases awareness of inauthentic patterns and creates opportunities for greater genuineness.

The "One More Layer" Technique:

When conversation remains superficial, practice going "one layer deeper" by:

- Sharing the "why" behind your stated opinions or preferences

- Adding a personal meaning dimension to factual information

- Expressing a feeling connected to the topic being discussed

This technique helps move beyond fact-only exchanges without jumping to inappropriate disclosure.

The Reciprocity Gauge:

Develop awareness of the vulnerability balance by noticing:

- Is one person doing most of the meaningful sharing?

- Does the other person respond to vulnerability with their own or change the subject faster than a cat losing interest in a toy?

- Does the depth of sharing feel mutually matched?

This awareness enables you to adjust your vulnerability level, fostering a balanced connection rather than one-sided exposure.

Elena transformed her dating approach with these techniques: "I used to either stay in safe, superficial conversation or occasionally share way too much when I felt insecure. Learning to consciously navigate vulnerability as a gradual, reciprocal process has completely changed the quality of the connections I create. I could feel the difference in how people responded to authentic sharing versus either my polished facade or my nervous oversharing."

Meaningful Conversation Techniques (Beyond "What Do You Do?")

We've all experienced the painful loop of small talk in dating: the same questions about work, hobbies, and Netflix shows that never seem to foster genuine understanding. It's like being stuck in a human resources interview that never ends. Meaningful conversations—creating authentic connections—require different approaches and skills.

Beyond "What Do You Do?": Conversation That Connects

Authentic connection develops through conversation beyond factual exchange to create shared meaning and understanding. This doesn't require heavy or intense topics—even lighthearted conversation can be meaningful when it reveals who you are rather than just what you do.

Research by Dr Matthias Mehl found that happier people have significantly more substantive conversations and fewer small talk exchanges. His studies showed that the depth of conversation was a better predictor of well-being than the number of social interactions, suggesting that quality truly matters more than quantity in social connection. (Finally, validation for introverts everywhere!)

The Art of Curious Questioning (Without Sounding Like an Interrogator)

The questions you ask have a profound impact on the connection you create. Most dating conversations rely on default questions that yield predictable, resume-style answers rather than genuine insight.

Transforming your questioning approach involves several shifts:

From Fact-Gathering to Perspective-Seeking:

- Instead of: "What do you do for work?"

- Try: "What do you find most meaningful about your work?" or "What's the strangest day you've had at your job?"

From Binary to Open Exploration:

- Instead of: "Did you like that movie?"

- Try: "What stood out to you about that movie?" or "What character did you relate to most?"

From Past Resume to Present Experience:

- Instead of: "Where did you go to school?"

- Try: "What's something you've been learning or curious about lately?" or "What's the most useful thing you ever learned outside of school?"

From General Abstractions to Specific Moments:

- Instead of: "Do you like travelling?"

- Try: "What's a travel moment that stayed with you?" or "What's the weirdest food you've tried while travelling?"

These shifts transform questions from data collection to invitations for authentic sharing.

Carlos noticed immediate changes when he altered his questioning approach: "I stopped asking the standard checklist questions and started asking about experiences, perspectives, and meanings. Suddenly, people were engaging in different ways—sharing stories and thoughts I'd never heard with my old approach. The conversations became genuinely interesting rather than feeling like interviews where I was trying to determine if they met my minimum requirements."

Listening That Creates Connection (Not Just Waiting for Your Turn to Talk)

Authentic connection requires not just better questions but transformed listening. Most people listen in one of three limited ways:

Autobiographical Listening:

Relating everything to your own experience:

- "That reminds me of when I..."

- "I had the same thing happen..."

- "That's just like my situation where..."

Solution Listening:

Jumping immediately to fix or advise:

- "What you should do is..."

- "Have you tried...?"

- "The problem is that you need to..."

Distracted Listening:

Being physically present but mentally elsewhere:

- Thinking about what you'll say next

- Checking notifications or scanning the room for someone more interesting

- Following tangential thoughts triggered by their words

None of these creates a genuine connection. Transformative listening involves a fundamentally different approach:

Presence Listening:

- Giving full attention without planning your response

- Noticing both content and emotional tone

- Being curious about their experience rather than comparing it to yours

- Allowing space for their complete expression before responding

Understanding-Focused Responses:

- "It sounds like that was important to you..."

- "I'm curious what that experience was like for you..."

- "What did that mean to you when it happened?"

Non-Verbal Connection:

- Maintaining appropriate eye contact (not serial killer staring, not constant phone checking)

- Offering affirming expressions and nods

- Physically orienting toward them

- Matching energy and tone appropriately

Mia transformed her dating experience by developing these listening skills: "I realised I'd been having adjacent monologues rather than conversations—just waiting for my turn to speak rather than truly listening. The quality of connection completely changed when I started giving people my full attention without immediately relating everything to myself. People opened up in ways they never had before, and I found myself genuinely interested in what they were saying instead of just pretending to be."

The Vulnerability-Curiosity Loop (It's Like a Good Feedback Loop, Not a Terrible Loop)

Authentic conversation creates what researchers call the "vulnerability-curiosity loop"—a powerful connection cycle where:

1. One person shares something authentically (vulnerability)

2. The other responds with genuine interest and understanding (curiosity)

3. This response creates safety for deeper sharing (increased vulnerability)

4. The deeper sharing prompts more meaningful exploration (increased curiosity)

This self-reinforcing cycle builds connection organically when both people participate. However, it breaks down if either vulnerability or curiosity is missing:

- Vulnerability without curiosity leads to one-sided sharing that feels unreciprocated

- Curiosity without vulnerability creates an interview dynamic rather than a mutual connection

Developing both skills—appropriate vulnerability and genuine curiosity—creates the conditions for this powerful connection cycle to develop naturally.

Navigating Conversation Roadblocks (Because Sometimes Things Get Awkward)

Even with strong connection skills, the conversation sometimes hits challenging spots. Developing techniques for these moments prevents disconnection:

For Conversational Lulls:

- Acknowledge the silence comfortably rather than rushing to fill it with nervous chatter

- Return to something mentioned earlier that could be explored more deeply

- Share an observation about the shared experience you're having

- Shift to a new topic with a thoughtful transition

For Potential Disagreements:

- Express curiosity about their perspective before asserting your own

- Acknowledge the valid aspects of their view even as you share differences

- Focus on understanding rather than persuading

- Find the shared values beneath differing opinions

For Sensitive Topics:

- Check whether it's an appropriate topic for your relationship stage

- Offer an "off-ramp" that allows either person to shift topics comfortably

- Share your own relevant experience before asking about theirs

- Express appreciation for their perspective regardless of the agreement

These navigation skills keep the conversation flowing authentically, even though challenging moments typically make you want to hide in the bathroom.

Exercise: The Escalating Intimacy Practice (No, Not THAT Kind of Intimacy)

This structured exercise helps you develop authentic connection skills progressively, building your capacity for meaningful interaction. It can be practised with friends before applying in dating contexts, making it a safe way to develop these abilities.

Preparation

Materials needed:

- A quiet setting without distractions

- 45-60 minutes of uninterrupted time

- A timer or clock

- The question sequence (provided below)

Mindset preparation:

- Commit to authentic responses rather than a polished presentation

- Agree to appropriate confidentiality about what's shared

- Adopt an attitude of curious exploration rather than performance

The Process

This exercise involves structured conversation that gradually increases in meaning and depth. Each person takes turns answering the same question before moving to the next level.

Level One: Low-Risk Sharing (15 minutes)

Exchange responses to these questions, spending about 3 minutes on each:

1. What's a small pleasure in your daily life that you particularly enjoy?

2. What are you curious about or interested in learning more about?

3. What place has special meaning for you, and what makes it significant?

4. If you had an entire day to yourself with no obligations, how would you spend it?

5. What's a quality you appreciate in the people you choose to have in your life?

Level Two: Value-Based Connection (15 minutes)

Move to slightly deeper questions that reveal more about your values and perspectives:

1. What have you changed your mind about in the last few years?

2. When do you feel most like yourself, and what factors contribute to that feeling?

3. What challenges have you faced that taught you something important?

4. What is something you stand for or strongly believe in?

5. How do you define success or a well-lived life for yourself?

Level Three: Meaningful Vulnerability (15 minutes)

If comfort and trust have developed, move to questions that invite appropriate vulnerability:

1. What are you working on or trying to improve about yourself?

2. When do you feel most misunderstood by others?

3. What relationship in your life has had the most impact on who you are today?

4. What's a fear or insecurity that sometimes influences your choices?

5. What's something you hope others see or understand about you?

Reflection Period (10 minutes)

After completing the questions, discuss the experience:

- What did you notice about the connection as the conversation progressed?

- Which questions created the strongest sense of understanding or resonance?

- What did you learn about creating meaningful conversations?

- How might this approach differ from your typical dating conversations?

Applying the Learning

After completing this exercise, identify specific elements you can incorporate into your dating approach:

- Question Transformation: Review your typical dating questions and transform 3-5 of them using the principles of this exercise.

- Listening Development: Based on your experience, identify one specific listening habit to change (e.g., reducing autobiographical responses, increasing curious follow-up).

- Vulnerability Calibration: Note where on the vulnerability spectrum you typically operate and set an intention for appropriate adjustment.

- Connection Awareness: Develop a simple way to check in with yourself during dates about the connection quality being created.

Sophia found this exercise transformative: "Practicing escalating intimacy with friends before dating helped me recognise what meaningful connection feels like. I realised my dating conversations had been stuck at Level One, with occasional inappropriate jumps to very personal disclosures. Learning to navigate the middle ground of values-based connection completely changed my dating experience."

Expert Interviews: Communication Specialists (Because Why Not Get Some Pro Tips?)

To provide deeper insight into authentic connections, I spoke with several specialists in interpersonal communication. Here are key perspectives from these conversations:

Dr. Rachel Martinez, Interpersonal Communication Researcher

"The biggest misconception about connection is that it happens spontaneously when you meet the 'right' person. Our research indicates that connection is a skill that can be developed through targeted practices and heightened awareness.

People often mistake chemistry for connection. Chemistry is a neurochemical reaction that may or may not lead to genuine understanding. True connection involves a mutual process of revealing and responding that builds over time. The good news is that, unlike largely automatic chemistry, the connection can be consciously cultivated."

On conversations that build relationships: "Our studies show that alternating disclosure—where each person progressively shares and responds—creates stronger bonds than either parallel monologues or question-answer dynamics.

The quality that most distinguishes connection-building conversation is what we call 'turned toward responses'. When one person shares something, and the other responds in a way that shows they've not just heard the words but understood their meaning and importance to the speaker, these responses create a sense of being 'gotten,' that forms the foundation of intimacy.

Marcus Lee, Dating Communication Coach

On vulnerability in early dating: "The biggest mistake I see is binary thinking—people are either wholly guarded or overshare inappropriately. Effective vulnerability is sequential and reciprocal.

I teach clients the 'disclosure step' approach—sharing one level more profound than the current conversation, then seeing if the other person meets you there. If they respond with similar depth, the connection deepens naturally. If they don't match your level after a couple of opportunities, that's valuable information about their readiness or interest in a genuine connection."

On authentic conversation starters: "The questions that create the most meaningful exchanges aren't about facts but about experiences and perspectives. Instead of asking what someone does, ask what drew them to their field or what they find most challenging. Instead of asking about hobbies, ask what state of mind or feeling those activities create.

These questions invite people to share not just information but meaning—and connection happens through meaning. The bonus is that these questions are more enjoyable for both parties, transforming dating from an interview mode to a genuine exploration."

Dr. Kim Jennings, Nonverbal Communication Expert

On the body language of authentic connection: "Our research using micro expression analysis shows that genuine connection has a distinct nonverbal signature different from polite interaction or attraction. Genuine connection involves synchronisation—matching of posture, gesture rhythm, and even breathing patterns.

The most telling nonverbal cue is 'whole-face engagement'—when someone's entire face, not just their mouth, responds to you. This includes the eyes (crow's feet crinkles in genuine smiles), the mid-face (raised cheeks), and the brow area (slight movement in response to emotions). People intuitively sense when this full facial engagement is present or absent."

"Creating a nonverbal connection: Authentic nonverbal connection cannot be faked, but it can be facilitated. Making complete eye contact, removing physical barriers between you, and intentionally putting away distractions create conditions where nonverbal synchrony can develop naturally.

The most potent practice is what we call 'embodied presence'— being fully in your body rather than in your analysing mind during interaction. This presence state allows your natural nonverbal expressiveness to emerge and creates the conditions for genuine nonverbal connection to develop."

Common Themes Across Expert Perspectives

Several key insights emerged consistently across these expert interviews:

1. Connection as Co-Creation: All experts emphasised that authentic connection is something people create together, not something that magically happens or doesn't based on compatibility.

2. The Progression Principle: Each highlighted the importance of progressive development rather than all-or-nothing approaches to openness and sharing.

3. Meaning Over Information: The distinction between exchanging information and creating shared meaning was central to all expert perspectives on connection.

4. The Presence Prerequisite: All experts identified full attention and presence as foundational requirements for developing a genuine connection.

5. The Reciprocity Requirement: Each emphasised that connection develops through mutual engagement rather than one-sided efforts, regardless of how skilled one person might be.

These themes provide a framework for understanding connection not as a mysterious chemistry but as a process that can be approached with awareness and skill.

The Continuous Connection Practice (Because This Isn't a One-and-Done Deal)

An authentic connection isn't achieved through a single conversation or technique—it's developed through consistent practice that gradually becomes natural. This section outlines a comprehensive approach to incorporating connection skills into your dating repertoire.

The Pre-Date Connection Preparation

Before the dates, many people focused exclusively on their appearance or planning impressive activities. Connection-focused preparation is different:

Presence Preparation:

- Schedule buffer time before dates to settle your nervous system (no rushing straight from work)

- Practice a brief centring exercise to bring yourself fully present

- Set an intention focused on connection rather than impression or outcome

- Release expectations and be open to discovering who this person truly is

Curiosity Cultivation:

- Develop 2-3 genuinely interesting questions relevant to what you know about them

- Create open-ended conversation starters that invite meaningful responses

- Reflect on what you're authentically curious about regarding this person

- Prepare yourself to listen for understanding rather than preparing your next witty comment

Authenticity Alignment:

- Check in with yourself about any masks or performances you tend to adopt

- Identify one aspect of yourself you often hide that could be appropriately shared

- Connect with your genuine interest in this connection beyond outcome concerns

- Notice any approval-seeking patterns and set an intention for authenticity

Carlos described how this preparation transformed his dating experience: "I spent all my pre-date time planning impressive things to say or rehearsing stories that made me look good. Now, I spend that time centring myself, getting curious about who I'm meeting, and connecting with my authentic intention. I arrive in a completely different state—present and open rather than anxious and performing."

The During-Date Connection Practices

Specific practices during dates can significantly enhance your connection capacity:

The Presence Reset:

When you notice your attention wandering or performance mode activating, practice this quick reset:

1. Take a single conscious breath

2. Feel your physical presence in your body

3. Re-engage with genuine curiosity

4. Listen with your full attention

This 5-second practice can transform the quality of interaction when done consistently.

The Meaningful Response Habit:

When the other person shares something, practice responding in ways that create a connection:

- Acknowledge both the content and the feeling behind what they shared

- Relate to the meaning rather than immediately sharing your similar experience

- Ask a follow-up question that invites deeper exploration

- Express appreciation for their sharing

The Authentic Expression Practice:

When sharing about yourself, develop the habit of:

- Checking whether you're expressing your genuine thoughts/feelings

- Include the "why" behind your statements to add meaning dimension

- Sharing appropriate vulnerabilities that reveal your authentic self

- Expressing what matters to you, not just what you do or have done

These practices transform everyday conversation into connection-building interaction.

The Post-Date Integration Process

After dates, most people focus on outcome assessment ("Do I like them? Do they like me?"). Connection-focused integration involves different questions:

Connection Quality Reflection:

- What moments of genuine connection did I experience during this interaction?

- When did I feel most authentic and present?

- What did I learn about creating or deepening connections?

- How did my connection practices affect the quality of our interaction?

Skill Development Assessment:

- Which connection skills did I implement effectively?

- Where did I notice myself falling into old patterns?

- What specific skill would enhance connection in future interactions?

- What did this particular person's style teach me about connection flexibility?

Integration Practice:

- Note specific insights about connections from this experience

- Identify one concrete practice to focus on in your next dating interaction

- Acknowledge growth in your connection capacity regardless of the dating outcome

- Connect these learnings to your broader relationship vision

This reflection process accelerates your connection skill development by extracting lessons from each dating experience.

The Progressive Development Approach

Like any complex skill set, an authentic connection develops through stages of mastery:

Stage 1: Conscious Implementation

In this initial stage, connection practices feel mechanical and require deliberate focus. You're consciously implementing specific techniques and noticing their effects. It's like learning to drive when you're still thinking "gas pedal, brake pedal, turn signal" for every move.

Stage 2: Comfortable Integration

As you practice consistently, individual techniques flow together more naturally. You still need to activate your connection practices intentionally, but they feel more integrated and less like separate techniques. This is like driving when you no longer have to think about each action but still need to pay attention.

Stage 3: Natural Embodiment

Eventually, connection skills become your default way of interacting rather than the special techniques you implement. Authentic presence, curiosity, and appropriate vulnerability become your natural state in dating interactions. At this point, you're like an experienced driver who can navigate complex situations while conversing.

Tanya described her progression: "At first, practising these connection skills felt like speaking a foreign language—I had to translate everything in my head before responding. It started feeling more natural after a few months of practice, though I still had to remind myself in nervous moments. Now, two years later, I can't imagine interacting any other way. It's just how I connect with people."

Customising Your Connection Approach (Because You're Uniquely You)

While the principles of authentic connection are universal, the practical application depends on honouring your unique personality and style:

For More Introverted People:

- Prioritize depth over breadth in conversation

- Allow yourself to process pauses when needed (and don't apologise for them!)

- Schedule dates in environments that support your energy style

- Recognize that thoughtful responses often create stronger connections than quick ones

For More Extroverted People:

- Channel your expressive energy into curious questions rather than just sharing

- Practice comfortable silence that creates space for a more profound exchange

- Notice when enthusiasm might be overwhelming quieter individuals

- Use your social comfort to create safety for meaningful exchange

For More Analytical People:

- Balance intellectual discussion with emotional and experiential sharing

- Notice opportunities to connect on feeling and meaning levels, not just ideas

- Use your analytical strength to notice patterns in connection

- Allow the conversation to flow beyond logical progression when appropriate

For More Emotional People:

- Balance feeling expression with a curious exploration of others' experience

- Create context for emotional sharing rather than assuming receptiveness

- Use your emotional intelligence to sense appropriate depth levels

- Provide structure for emotional sharing that enhances rather than overwhelms connection

The goal isn't to become someone you're not but to express your authentic self in ways that create meaningful connections. The most powerful connections happen when you bring your genuine nature to the interaction, enhanced by skills that bridge the gap between people.

When Connection Doesn't Develop (Sometimes It's Just Not There)

Sometimes, despite your best efforts, an authentic connection doesn't emerge with a particular person. This isn't necessarily a skill failure but is often a matter of compatibility.

Signs that connection limitations may be about compatibility rather than technique:

- You consistently implement connection practices with limited response

- The other person seems uncomfortable with deeper conversation

- Attempts at meaningful exchange are repeatedly redirected to superficial topics

- You feel yourself working very hard to maintain the connection

- The interaction consistently returns to performance mode despite your efforts

In these situations, recognise that not every pairing has the capacity for deep connection, regardless of skills. Some connections remain pleasant but superficial due to differences in:

- Communication styles

- Emotional openness capacity

- Connection values and priorities

- Current readiness for authentic engagement

Rather than forcing a connection or blaming yourself when it doesn't develop, view these experiences as valuable information about compatibility. The goal of authentic connection skills isn't to connect deeply with everyone but to create the conditions where meaningful connections can flourish when essential compatibility exists.

As you continue your dating journey with these enhanced connection skills, remember that authentic connection isn't just a means to a relationship end—it's a fundamental human need and value in itself. Each genuine connection, whether it leads to a lasting relationship or not, enriches your life and enhances your ability to form meaningful relationships.

The skills you're developing will serve you not just in finding a partner but in creating depth in all your relationships. The capacity for authentic connection is perhaps the most valuable relationship skill you can develop—one that will enhance every interaction and create the foundation for the profoundly fulfilling relationship you seek.

In the next chapter, we'll explore how to evaluate compatibility once the connection has been established, ensuring you can distinguish between genuine alignment and merely enjoyable company (because sometimes chemistry is just chemistry, not compatibility!).

CHAPTER 10:

Evaluating Compatibility

Beyond Chemistry: The Four Pillars of Compatibility

So you've met someone. There's that spark. Conversation flows like a good wine on a Friday night. You find yourself checking your phone more often than a teenager with a new crush. But is this the beginning of something meaningful, or just another situationship that feels promising but will leave you watching sad movies and eating ice cream straight from the container in a month?

This, my friend, is where intentional compatibility assessment becomes your new best friend. While chemistry creates that initial "oh hello there" moment, compatibility determines whether your relationship thrives or takes a nosedive when the honeymoon phase ends.

Think of chemistry as the ignition that starts your relationship engine, while compatibility is the fuel that keeps it running. Without both, your journey together won't last—either it never starts (no chemistry), or it stalls out somewhere between "meeting the parents" and "whose turn is it to do the dishes" (no compatibility).

The problem? Most of us rely on that magical feeling of "clicking" to assess compatibility, which is about as reliable as using a Magic 8-Ball to plan your retirement. As relationship researcher Dr Ted Huston puts it: "The feelings we interpret as compatibility are often just familiarity, projection, or biochemical attraction—none of which predict actual relationship success."

Time for a better approach: assessing compatibility across four fundamental dimensions—the Four Pillars of Compatibility. No, this isn't another personality test that will tell you you're an "INFJ with Ravenclaw tendencies." This is the practical stuff that actually matters.

Pillar 1: Values Compatibility

(Or: Do You Want the Same Big Stuff in Life?)

Values are your core principles and priorities—the beliefs guiding your significant life decisions and defining what matters most. Values compatibility doesn't mean you need to be identical twins who agree on everything from politics to how to load the dishwasher. It means alignment on the fundamental principles that shape how you approach life.

Key Value Areas to Assess:

- **Life Direction Values:** How you define success, growth, and purpose. Does "making it" mean a corner office or a cabin in the woods?

- **Ethical Values:** Core principles about right and wrong. Is honesty always the best policy, or are white lies sometimes necessary?

- **Relationship Values:** Beliefs about how relationships should function. Is marriage a must or just a piece of paper?

- **Family Values:** Perspectives on family roles, parenting, and dynamics. Will holidays be a Norman Rockwell painting or a chaotic free-for-all?

- **Financial Values:** Attitudes toward money, security, and resources. Save for a rainy day or live for the moment?

- **Spiritual Values:** Beliefs about meaning, spirituality, and existential questions. Sunday church or Sunday brunch?

Here's the kicker: value compatibility is evident through stated beliefs and actual behaviours. That date, who claims family is everything but hasn't spoken to their parents in years? Pay attention to that disconnect. Watch how potential partners make decisions, prioritise when stressed, and treat the barista who messed up their order—these behaviours reveal values more accurately than their dating profile ever will.

Elena discovered a significant values incompatibility with someone she was dating when discussing future goals: "He casually mentioned that his five-year plan was to build enough wealth to retire early, even if it meant working 80 hours a week until then. I value work-life balance and presence over maximum financial gain. Neither approach is wrong, but they're fundamentally incompatible visions of life."

Pillar 2: Emotional Compatibility

(Or: How You Handle the Feels)

Emotional compatibility involves how you and a potential partner experience, express and respond to feelings. This isn't about having identical emotional styles—one of you can be a crier during sad movies while the other stays stoic. What matters is whether your emotional approaches work harmoniously together.

Key Emotional Compatibility Factors:

- **Emotional Expression Styles:** How openly and intensely emotions are expressed. Are they a walking emoji or more of a poker face?

- **Emotional Regulation Approaches:** How each person manages complicated feelings. Deep breaths, long walks, or slam doors?

- **Support Preferences:** How each gives and receives emotional support. Do they need a problem-solver or just a good listener?

- **Conflict Styles:** How disagreements and hurt feelings are handled. Cool-down period, or hash it out immediately?

- **Intimacy Comfort:** Ease with emotional closeness and vulnerability. Are they an open book or more of a classified document?

- **Emotional Intelligence:** Ability to recognise and respond to emotions appropriately. Can they read the room, or are they emotionally tone-deaf?

Emotional compatibility often reveals itself during challenging moments. Notice how you feel after disagreements—do you eventually feel closer through resolution, or do you feel like you've just gone ten rounds in an emotional boxing match?

Marcus realised his emotional compatibility with his date during an unexpected situation: "Our dinner reservation was lost, and it was pouring rain. I tend to get irritable in these situations, but instead of getting annoyed with my reaction, she acknowledged my frustration, suggested a practical alternative, and maintained a calm presence. Our different but complementary emotional styles helped us navigate the challenge together rather than escalating it."

Pillar 3: Practical/Lifestyle Compatibility

(Or: Can You Stand Each Other's Day-to-Day Habits?)

This pillar concerns the tangible, day-to-day aspects of life. Perhaps less romantic to consider than soulmate connections, but it's the difference between "happily ever after" and "I can't live with your habit of leaving wet towels on the bed for ONE MORE DAY."

Key Practical Compatibility Areas:

- **Daily Rhythms:** Sleep schedules, energy patterns, and routine preferences. Early bird or night owl?

- **Living Preferences:** Organization, cleanliness, and home environment. Is a little mess "homey", or does it trigger your anxiety?

- **Leisure Time:** How free time is spent and valued. Netflix marathon or hiking adventure?

- **Social Preferences:** Introversion/extroversion and social needs. Party every weekend or quiet dinners at home?

- **Health Approaches:** Attitudes toward fitness, nutrition, and well-being. Gym rat or couch potato?

- **Financial Habits:** Spending, saving, and financial management styles. Budget tracker or "What's a budget?"

These practical matters might seem minor during early dating but become increasingly significant once the relationship progresses beyond "I'll just go home to my place when you start leaving your dishes in the sink."

After several dates, Sophia noticed a practical compatibility issue: "He mentioned constantly having friends stay at his place without planning, describing his home as a 'crash pad' for his extensive social circle. I need my home to be a peaceful sanctuary with planned social interactions. This difference seemed minor at first, but I realised it would create daily friction in a serious relationship."

Pillar 4: Physical/Sexual Compatibility

(Or: Is There Long-Term Spark?)

Physical compatibility extends beyond whether you find each other hot. It includes alignment in physical affection needs, sexual preferences, and overall physical connection. While this area can develop and adapt over time, fundamental misalignment can create significant relationship strain. (Yes, we need to talk about this stuff, adults.)

Key Physical Compatibility Factors:

- **Affection Styles:** Preferences for touch, closeness, and non-sexual physical connection. Cuddler or need-my-space?

- **Sexual Desires:** Alignment in drive, preferences, and interests. Similar appetites or significant differences?

- **Physical Communication:** Ability to express needs and respond to feedback. Can you talk about what works and what doesn't?

- **Body Boundaries:** Respect and understanding of physical boundaries. Are limits acknowledged and honoured?

- **Health Approaches:** Compatibility in attitudes toward physical health and care. Aligned on self-care practices?

- **Attraction Sustainability:** Ongoing physical interest beyond initial chemistry. Is it just "new relationship energy" or deeper attraction?

Physical compatibility becomes apparent gradually as the relationship develops. Notice not just the presence of attraction but also how comfortable the physical connection feels—compatibility manifests as both desire and ease.

Carlos recognised his partner's physical compatibility in subtle ways: "Beyond the obvious attraction, I noticed how naturally we found our physical rhythm—from how we hugged to how we moved around each other in the kitchen. There was an unforced physical harmony that made all kinds of touch feel natural rather than awkward."

The Compatibility Assessment Matrix

(Not Nearly as Boring as It Sounds)

The key to practical compatibility evaluation is assessing all four pillars independently rather than letting strength in one area mask weakness in others. It's like evaluating a car—great acceleration doesn't compensate for faulty brakes.

Common assessment mistakes include:

- Letting strong physical chemistry override significant values incompatibility (The "But we're so good together... in bed" trap)

- Assuming emotional connection guarantees practical compatibility (The "Love conquers all... except your terrible financial habits" delusion)

- Overlooking values differences because daily interactions are pleasant (The "We'll cross that bridge when we get to it" postponement)

- Minimizing physical compatibility concerns due to strong alignment in other areas (The "Physical stuff isn't that important anyway" rationalisation)

To avoid these pitfalls, try using a simple matrix approach. After several dates, rate compatibility in each pillar from 1-10, considering:

- **Alignment:** How well your approaches/needs/beliefs match or complement each other

- **Adaptation:** How easily differences could be bridged through mutual growth

- **Importance:** How crucial this particular pillar is to your relationship vision

This structured assessment helps you see potential relationships more clearly rather than through the distorting lens of chemistry or wishful thinking.

Maya used this approach after repeatedly being drawn to physically compatible partners while ignoring value incompatibility: "The matrix made me face reality. With Tyler, I rated our physical compatibility 9/10 but values compatibility only 4/10. Seeing the numbers in black and white helped me acknowledge this wasn't a minor issue but a fundamental mismatch, despite our chemistry."

Red Flags vs. Growth Opportunities

(Or: Deal-Breakers vs. Growing Pains)

One of the most challenging distinctions when evaluating potential partners is between red flags that signal fundamental incompatibility and typical differences that represent growth opportunities. This confusion often leads people to either bail on promising relationships prematurely or stay in unsuitable ones until they've memorised all the lyrics to every breakup song ever written.

Understanding True Red Flags

Red flags are warning signs that indicate potentially serious problems in a relationship's future. They're not merely annoying habits or differences but indicators of:

- Fundamental value incompatibilities

- Harmful relationship patterns

- Character issues that threaten relationship health

- Problems unlikely to change significantly over time

The most reliable red flags tend to fall into several categories:

Respect Issues:

- Consistent boundary violations, even after discussion ("I know you said no drop-ins, but I was in the neighbourhood...")

- Disrespectful treatment of service workers or others with less power (The classic "rude to the waiter" test)

- Dismissiveness toward your thoughts, feelings, or experiences ("You're overreacting," "It's not that big a deal")

- Different standards for their behaviour versus yours ("It's fine when I do it, but not when you do")

Honesty Concerns:

- Pattern of even "small" lies or misrepresentations ("White lies" that form a pattern)

- Significant information withheld until confronted ("Oh, did I forget to mention my three kids and ongoing divorce?")

- Inconsistency between words and actions (Says one thing, does another)

- Deflection or defensiveness when questioned (Can never admit being wrong)

Emotional Patterns:

- Inability to take responsibility for emotional impact ("That's just how I am")

- Extreme emotional reactions to minor situations (Zero to sixty over small issues)

- Using emotions manipulatively to control outcomes (Crying or anger as manipulation tactics)

- Consistent blaming of others for personal problems (The world is against them)

Control Behaviours:

- Subtle or overt attempts to direct your choices (From clothing to friendships)

- Isolation tactics that separate you from support systems ("Your friends don't like me")

- Unpredictable responses that keep you walking on eggshells (Never know which version will show up)

- Using affection or approval as rewards for compliance (Love becomes conditional)

Jason ignored several control-related red flags because his date was otherwise attentive and affectionate: "She had strong opinions about my clothes, friends, and how I spent my time—always framed as 'just wanting the best for me.' I mistook this for caring until my therapist helped me see these weren't preferences but control patterns that would likely escalate over time."

Identifying Growth Opportunities

Unlike red flags, growth opportunities are differences or challenges that:

- Can potentially strengthen the relationship through mutual effort

- Represent normal human imperfections rather than fundamental flaws

- Provide opportunities for both partners to develop and stretch

- Show potential for positive change over time

Signs that a challenge might be a growth opportunity rather than a red flag:

Awareness and Ownership:

- The person recognises the issue without excessive defensiveness

- They take responsibility rather than blame or deflect

- There's evidence of previous personal growth in other areas

- They can discuss the challenge reflectively rather than reactively

Effort and Progress:

- You see active efforts to address the issue, not just promises

- There's an observable improvement, even if inconsistent

- The person seeks to understand the impact of their behaviour

- They welcome appropriate support in making changes

Willingness to Engage:

- They're open to feedback without shutting down or attacking

- There's the willingness to seek outside help (books, therapy, etc.)

- They initiate conversations about improvement, not just respond to complaints

- The issue doesn't represent their core values or identity

Sophia recognised a growth opportunity with her partner around communication styles: "We had different approaches to discussing problems—I process verbally while he needs time to think before responding. Initially, I interpreted his silence as a form of avoidance, but I noticed how he would thoughtfully return to topics after reflection and was actively working on giving me interim responses while he processed. His awareness and effort showed this was a growth area, not a red flag."

The Adaptation Question

When assessing whether differences represent red flags or growth opportunities, consider what adaptation would be required from each person:

Healthy Adaptation: Learning new skills, expanding comfort zones, developing greater understanding, finding creative compromises

Unhealthy Adaptation: Suppressing core needs, violating personal values, accepting disrespect, diminishing identity, continuous one-sided compromise

Elena realised a difference with her partner required unhealthy adaptation: "He believed partners should share all their thoughts and feelings immediately, while I need processing time before discussing emotional matters. He viewed my need for reflection as 'secretive' and pressured me to change this fundamental aspect of how I function emotionally. I realised this wasn't a growth opportunity but a request to adapt in a way that would harm my wellbeing."

The Assessment Framework

To distinguish red flags from growth opportunities, assess challenges along four dimensions:

1. Pattern vs. Incident

- Is this a one-time occurrence or a recurring pattern?

- Has this behaviour been observed in various situations or relationships?

- Is the behaviour consistent or situational?

2. Awareness vs. Blindness

- Does the person recognise the issue without external pressure?

- Can they articulate the impact of their behaviour?

- Do they demonstrate genuine understanding rather than merely intellectual acknowledgement?

3. Willingness vs. Resistance

- How does the person respond to feedback about the issue?
- Are they proactively addressing the challenge or minimising it?
- Do they demonstrate commitment to growth in this area?

4. Progress vs. Stagnation

- Is there observable improvement over time?
- Are lapses becoming less frequent or severe?
- Does addressing the issue feel like a shared journey or a constant battle?

Challenges that exhibit patterns, blindness, resistance, and stagnation typically serve as red flags. Those characterised by isolated incidents, awareness, willingness, and progress are more likely to represent growth opportunities.

When to Stay and When to Move On

(The Million-Dollar Question)

Despite our best assessment efforts, one of the most challenging aspects of dating is deciding when to continue investing in a connection versus acknowledging incompatibility and moving on. This decision becomes particularly difficult when a relationship has positive and negative elements. It's like trying to decide whether to keep watching a show that has amazing moments but also frustrating plot holes.

The Common Decision Traps

Several psychological tendencies make this decision particularly difficult:

The Sunk Cost Fallacy The tendency to continue a relationship based on how much you've already invested rather than its future potential. This manifests as thoughts like:

- "We've been dating for three months already..."
- "I've already introduced them to my friends and family..."
- "I've put a lot of effort into making this work..."

The Potential Fixation Focusing on what someone could become rather than who they currently are:

- "They have so much potential if they would only..."
- "Once they get through this difficult period, they'll be able to..."

- "They're nearly perfect except for this one thing..."

The Scarcity Mindset The fear that better options aren't available leads to thoughts like:

- "What if I never find someone else?"

- "At least they have these good qualities..."

- "Dating is so difficult—this might be as good as it gets..."

The Perfectionism Pendulum Swinging between unrealistic expectations and settling for serious incompatibilities:

- "No relationship is perfect, so I should accept these problems..."

- "I'm being too picky if I end things over these concerns..."

- "Maybe my standards are unreasonably high..."

Carlos was caught in the sunk cost fallacy: "After five months of dating someone with fundamentally different values, I kept thinking about all the time I'd invested and how much my friends liked her. My therapist asked a clarifying question: 'If you had just met her today, knowing what you know now, would you start dating her?' The immediate 'no' made my decision clear."

The Stay or Go Assessment

While there's no perfect formula for this decision, a structured assessment helps cut through emotional confusion. Consider these key questions:

Fundamental Compatibility:

- Are your core values fundamentally aligned or in conflict?

- Can you envision a daily life together that works for both of you?

- Do you bring out the best in each other more often than not?

- Can you be authentically yourself in the relationship?

Problem Trajectory:

- Are concerning issues improving or worsening over time?

- Do conversations about problems lead to positive change?

- Are both individuals actively working on areas for growth?

- Is the overall trend moving toward greater understanding?

Balance Assessment:

- Does the relationship bring more positive elements to your life than negative ones?

- Is effort in the relationship relatively balanced between both people?

- Can you be both honest and kind with each other during difficulties?

- Do you feel energised or depleted after time together?

Future Orientation:

- Can you imagine a fulfilling future with this person as they are now?

- Would that future align with your most important life goals?

- Would being with this person facilitate or hinder your personal growth?

- Can you respect who they are fundamentally, not just who they could become?

Maya used this assessment after two months of dating someone with strong initial chemistry but emerging concerns: "The compatibility was questionable, problems persisted despite discussions, the relationship was becoming energetically depleting, and I couldn't honestly envision a future together without major changes on his part. Seeing these answers lined up, I decided to end things clearly despite the chemistry."

The Relationship Math Equation

Relationship mathematician Dr Hannah Fry suggests a clarifying framework she calls the "37% rule," based on the theory of optimal stopping. While somewhat tongue-in-cheek, the underlying principle is sound:

The question isn't "Is this person perfect?" but rather "Is this person better than the alternatives?"

The alternatives include:

- Potential future partners you might meet
- The quality of life you would have while single
- The relationship you might build with someone more compatible

This perspective helps counter the "bird in hand" fallacy that keeps people in mediocre relationships out of fear of the unknown.

Jason applied this thinking to his dating situation: "I realised I was settling for a connection that was just 'fine' because it felt safer than being single again. When I assessed whether this relationship was better than my contented single life and the possibility of meeting someone more compatible, the answer was no. That clarity helped me make a decision I'd been avoiding."

The 3-2-1 Decision Method

For particularly difficult decisions, try this structured approach:

3 Perspective Shifts:

- How would you advise your best friend in this exact situation?
- How will you likely view this relationship five years from now?
- If you were starting over today, would you choose this person again?

2 Core Questions:

- Does this relationship bring out your best self or your survival self?
- Is staying motivated more by possibility or by fear?

1 Gut Check:

- If all external pressures and opinions disappeared, what would you choose?

This method helps break through emotional confusion by approaching the decision from multiple angles.

Tanya found clarity through this process: "When I imagined advising my best friend in my situation, I immediately knew I'd tell her to move on—the values incompatibility was too fundamental. That perspective shift cut through months of confusion and helped me make a confident decision."

The Trial Separation Clarity Test

A brief, intentional separation period can clarify if you remain genuinely uncertain after a thorough assessment. This isn't a "break" to date others but a deliberate pause to:

- Experience how you feel with distance from the relationship
- Notice which aspects you miss and which bring relief
- Reduce emotional intensity to enable clearer thinking
- Assess the relationship's impact on your overall wellbeing

To be effective, this separation should:

- Have a specific timeframe (typically 2-4 weeks)
- Include clear boundaries about contact
- Have an explicit purpose of assessment rather than punishment
- End with a decision rather than default continuation

Many people report that even a week of intentional separation brings remarkable clarity about whether a relationship fits. Sometimes distance does make the heart grow fonder—or make you realise you're sleeping better than you have in months.

Exercise: The Three-Date Assessment Method

(Your Dating Detective Kit)

Early dating offers a crucial window for assessing compatibility before emotional attachment complicates the objective evaluation. The Three-Date Assessment Method offers a structured approach to gathering and evaluating key compatibility information within the first three dates.

While three dates aren't always enough for a complete assessment, this timeframe provides sufficient information for an initial compatibility evaluation while limiting premature emotional investment. Think of it as dating with your eyes open instead of letting those heart-shaped glasses fog your judgment.

First Date: Values and Basic Connection

The first date focuses on foundational elements:

Observation Focus:

- Communication basics (listening, reciprocity, interest)
- Value indicators in conversation and behaviour
- Treatment of others (e.g., service staff)
- Basic manners and respect
- Initial comfort and authenticity

Key Questions to Explore:

- What matters to them and why?

- How do they talk about previous relationships?

- What are their relationships like with family and friends?

- What are they passionate or excited about?

- How do they make decisions in their life?

Post-Date Reflection Questions:

- Did I feel comfortable and respected?

- Could I be reasonably authentic, or did I need to put on a show?

- Did I notice any significant value misalignments?

- Was there essential reciprocity in conversation and interest?

- Did I see any concerning red flags in behaviour or attitude?

- Is there enough potential to warrant a second date?

The first date assessment isn't about perfect alignment but about establishing whether essential compatibility and respect exist to justify further exploration.

Marcus used this framework effectively: "On a first date, she made several dismissive comments about her 'annoying religious family' and seemed irritated when I mentioned spirituality was important to me. Before this method, I might have overlooked it, focusing on our chemistry. Instead, I recognised this as a potential core values misalignment that warranted attention on a second date."

Second Date: Emotional and Lifestyle Compatibility

The second date builds on essential connection to explore deeper compatibility areas:

Observation Focus:

- Emotional expression and regulation
- Daily lifestyle patterns and preferences
- Conflict style indicators
- Energy compatibility between you
- Greater comfort and authenticity

Key Questions to Explore:

- How do they structure their typical day and week?
- What do they do to relax or handle stress?
- How do they describe their approach to communication?
- What are their hopes or plans for the next few years?

- How do they handle frustration or disappointment?

Post-Date Reflection Questions:

- How did our energy and pace align or differ?

- Did I notice compatibility in how we express and respond to emotions?

- Could I imagine integrating this person's lifestyle with mine?

- How did they respond to any moments of disagreement or tension?

- Has authentic conversation developed, or does it remain superficial?

- Do I feel more comfortable than after the first date?

The second date assessment looks for emerging patterns rather than isolated behaviours, focusing on how your lifestyles and emotional approaches might mesh over time.

Sophia applied this framework on her second date: "I noticed he changed the subject whenever I shared anything emotional, steering the conversation back to intellectual topics. When I gently pointed this out, he seemed genuinely surprised and explained that his family rarely discussed feelings. His awareness and willingness to discuss this pattern suggested a growth opportunity rather than a compatibility dealbreaker."

Third Date: Projection and Integration

The third date moves toward future compatibility assessment:

Observation Focus:

- How do you feel in their presence beyond the initial chemistry
- Their behaviour in different settings than previous dates
- Consistency across the three encounters
- Beginning signs of patterns in the connection
- Greater depth of conversation and sharing

Key Questions to Explore:

- What does their ideal relationship look like day-to-day?
- How have they grown or changed in recent years?
- What would they like to improve about themselves?
- How do they handle conflict in relationships?
- What are their non-negotiables in partnerships?

Post-Date Reflection Questions:

- Can I imagine building a life with this person as they are now?

- Do their relationship expectations seem compatible with mine?

- Have I seen consistent positive traits across all interactions?

- How do I feel about myself when I'm with this person?

- Have any red flags appeared that concern me?

- Do I want to continue investing in this connection?

The third-date assessment integrates observations across all three encounters to evaluate emerging patterns and compatibility indicators.

Elena found clarity through this process: "After three thoughtfully assessed dates, I realised we had strong intellectual chemistry but significantly different emotional needs. He preferred autonomous processing during stress, while I needed active verbal support. Neither approach is wrong, but recognising this fundamental difference early helped me make an informed decision about compatibility before strong attachment developed."

Research Spotlight: What Actually Predicts Relationship Success?

Understanding what predicts relationship success can significantly improve your compatibility assessment. Decades of relationship research have identified factors that consistently predict relationship longevity and satisfaction beyond the usual suspects of attraction and shared interests.

The Gottman Findings

Dr. John Gottman's groundbreaking research, which followed couples for over 40 years, identified several powerful predictors of relationship success:

Friendship Foundation Couples with strong friendship components—characterised by fondness, admiration, and detailed knowledge of each other's worlds—showed significantly higher relationship stability. This "deep friendship" proved more predictive of longevity than passion or frequency of conflict. The couples who could tell you their partner's favourite movie, current work challenge, or childhood dream were still happily together decades later.

Repair Capability Effectively repairing connections after conflict or disconnection predicted relationship success with over 90% accuracy. Interestingly, successful couples didn't have fewer conflicts but demonstrated more effective repair processes when disputes arose. It's not about never fighting but knowing how to make up afterwards.

Positivity Ratio Relationships that maintained a ratio of at least 5:1 of positive to negative interactions, even during conflict discussions, showed dramatically higher stability rates. This "emotional bank account" of positive interactions buffered relationships during inevitable challenging periods. In other words, you need five genuine compliments to counteract one: "Who left the milk out AGAIN?!"

Influence Acceptance Partners who showed a willingness to be influenced by each other's perspectives and needs demonstrated much higher relationship satisfaction and longevity than those with rigid positions, regardless of other compatibility factors. The ability to say "you know what, you might be right" turns out to be relationship gold.

Shared Meaning System Couples who created and maintained shared meaning around life goals, values, and symbols showed greater resilience to stressors and higher overall satisfaction. This "shared meaning" provided a larger context that helped weather day-to-day challenges. Whether it's a shared faith, political vision, or commitment to a particular lifestyle, having a "bigger why" helps relationships endure.

Practical Tool: Your Compatibility Evaluation Toolkit

As you apply these compatibility assessment approaches to your dating life, remember that the goal isn't perfect compatibility (which doesn't exist outside of rom-coms) but sufficient alignment in the areas that matter most for relationship health.

Every relationship involves differences and challenges—the question is whether the differences between you and a potential partner can be navigated through mutual growth and adaptation or if there are fundamental incompatibilities that would require unhealthy compromise.

Improving your compatibility assessment skills increases the likelihood of finding a suitable partner for a lasting relationship. It's not about finding someone perfect—it's about finding someone perfect for you, with whom you can build something that lasts beyond the initial excitement.

So the next time you feel those butterflies with someone new, enjoy them—but then put on your detective hat and start looking for the compatibility clues that will tell you if this particular butterfly effect might last beyond the honeymoon phase. Your future self (and your future therapist) will thank you.

CHAPTER 11:

From Dating to Relationship

Navigating the Awkward Middle Space (Without Losing Your Mind)

Congratulations! You've done the work. You've taken your dating sabbatical, reconnected with your true self, dated strategically instead of desperately, and found someone with genuine compatibility. No small feat in the age of dating apps and ghosting!

Now, you're entering what might be the most exciting—and surprisingly tricky—phase of your relationship journey: the transition from dating to a committed relationship. And no, changing your Facebook status doesn't count as "handling the transition." (Though we'll take the dopamine hit from those likes!)

This transition isn't just a formality or a box to check. Think of it as pouring the foundation for your relationship house. Get it right, and you'll build something sturdy enough to withstand life's hurricanes. Rush it, and, well... let's just say there's a reason why so many relationships develop cracks during their first real challenge.

Welcome to Relationship Limbo

You know that awkward feeling when you're not quite sure if you should introduce this person as "someone I'm seeing" or "my partner"? When you're toggling between casual and committed in your own mind? Congratulations—you've entered what sociologists call a "liminal space"—that threshold between two established states.

You're in transition territory when:

- Your date nights have morphed from "getting to know you" to "building something together"

- You're starting to make future plans (beyond next Friday's dinner)

- You've had at least one "Wait, are we exclusive?" thought

- You've considered introducing them to your friends (the nice ones first, obviously)

- You feel both exhilarated and occasionally panicked about where this is going

As Elena put it perfectly: "We were past the getting-to-know-you phase but hadn't yet had explicit conversations about what we were building. It felt like relationship limbo—more than just dating, but without clear agreements about what that meant for us."

This transition typically happens after 1-4 months of consistent dating, though everyone moves at their own pace (and that's okay—this isn't a race).

The Transition Traps That'll Get You Every Time

Before we get to the good stuff, let's talk about the potholes that can turn your smooth relationship road into a suspension-destroying mess:

The Assumption Trap

This is when both people make wildly different assumptions about relationship status, expectations, and boundaries without actually talking about it. Like Carlos, who learned the hard way: "I assumed exclusivity after two months, while she assumed we were still free to date others until we had a specific conversation. We were operating under completely different relationship rules without realising it—cue unnecessary heartbreak."

The Intensity Override

Remember those delicious brain chemicals flooding your system? They feel amazing but can override rational thinking faster than a sugar rush at a candy factory. Mia recognised this pattern: "The transition period always felt amazing because of the neurochemical high. I'd rush into commitments based on those feelings, then be shocked when reality hit a few months later, and I realised we hadn't built anything solid underneath all those good feelings."

The Identity Compromise

This is the subtle art of becoming a relationship chameleon—changing your colours to match what you think your partner wants. Jason caught himself in the act: "As things got more serious, I realised I was holding back opinions that differed from hers and downplaying interests she didn't share. I was unconsciously trying to be her perfect match rather than my authentic self."

The Clarity-Connection Paradox

This frustrating dynamic emerges when one person needs clear labels to feel safe deepening the connection, while the other needs to feel the deeper connection before offering those labels. It's a relationship between chicken and egg. Sophia navigated this challenge: "I needed to know where we stood before fully opening my heart, while he felt he needed more time to develop the connection before defining the relationship. Understanding this difference helped us avoid what could have been a painful standoff."

The External Timing Pressure

When everyone from your mom to your Instagram followers starts asking "So are you two official yet?" creating artificial pressure that rushes the process. Alex felt this acutely: "Everyone kept asking if we were 'official.' Family wanted to know if they should include her in holiday plans. Friends referred to her as my girlfriend before we'd defined things that way. All this external pressure made it hard to progress at our natural pace."

The Intentional Transition: A Better Way Forward

Instead of rushing through or sleepwalking through this crucial period, try the intentional approach. Think of it as mindful relationship building (without the meditation app subscription):

1. **Acknowledge the Transition**: Name it! "Hey, it feels like we're entering a new phase here. Let's talk about that."

2. **Have Actual Conversations** About expectations, hopes, concerns, and needs. Yes, using actual words, not telepathy (still not a thing, despite what romantic comedies suggest).

3. **Progress Gradually**: Build commitment in intentional steps rather than making the binary leap from "dating" to "practically married."

4. **Foundation First**: Focus on establishing relationship fundamentals before increasing practical entanglements (like adopting that cute puppy together).

5. **Check In Regularly**: Don't assume you're on the same page—confirm it.

Maya and her partner nailed this approach: "We explicitly acknowledged we were entering a transition phase and had several conversations about what that meant for each of us. Instead of making assumptions, we discussed everything from communication expectations to how we'd handle disagreements. It wasn't always comfortable—deep conversations rarely are—but it created clarity and connection that strengthened our relationship."

Building a Foundation That Won't Collapse Under Pressure

The transition period is your golden opportunity to establish core elements that support long-term relationship health. Think of it as relationship infrastructure—not the sexy part of the building, but the part that keeps it from falling down.

The Communication Foundation

How you communicate now tends to become your default pattern, so establish healthy habits early:

Transparency Practices Create norms for sharing thoughts and feelings without fear of judgment:

- Regular check-ins about relationship development

- Comfort expressing both positive and challenging emotions

- Proactive sharing rather than having to play detective

Emma and her partner created a weekly "relationship temperature check": "Every Sunday evening, we share what felt good that week and what could use attention. This simple practice made talking about our relationship normal rather than something that only happens during arguments."

Conflict Navigation Approach Develop patterns for handling disagreements before you have a major fight:

- Identify your different conflict styles (Are you a fighter? A freezer? A flee-er?)

- Create agreements about productive disagreement

- Establish repair rituals for after disconnections

Jordan focused on this foundation: "Early in our transition, we disagreed about social plans. Instead of just resolving that specific issue, we discussed how we wanted to handle conflicts in general. This conversation set a pattern of approaching disagreements as 'us against the problem' rather than 'me against you.'"

Meta-Communication Learn to talk about how you talk to each other (yes, it's communication inception):

- Notice and name communication patterns

- Adjust approaches based on what actually works

- Discuss communication needs and preferences

Tyler found this transformative: "We realised I process things internally before speaking, while she processes by talking things through. Instead of this becoming a source of friction, we discussed it directly and found ways to accommodate both styles. This prevented so many potential misunderstandings."

The Boundaries Foundation

Healthy relationships need both connection AND appropriate separation:

Individual Identity Maintenance Create norms that support continued individual development:

- Maintain meaningful individual friendships and activities

- Support personal goals and aspirations

- Preserve alone time and personal space

Aisha prioritised this: "During our transition, we explicitly discussed the importance of maintaining our separate identities. We each identified non-negotiable personal activities and supported each other in preserving them, which prevented the co-dependency I'd experienced before."

Relationship Boundaries Establish agreements about what stays within the relationship:

- Privacy expectations regarding relationship details

- Approach to social media sharing

- Handling of sensitive personal information

Carlos established clear boundaries: "We discussed what aspects of our relationship were private versus what we were comfortable sharing with friends or family. This created safety to be vulnerable with each other without worrying how that vulnerability might be shared outside our relationship."

External Relationship Management Develop approaches for navigating relationships with family, friends, exes, and others:

- Integration pace with existing social circles

- Boundaries with opposite-sex friendships

- Expectations regarding family involvement

Sarah focused on this: "We both had complex family dynamics that had created problems in previous relationships. During our transition, we discussed how we'd approach family interactions, what support we needed around difficult family members, and how to present a united front while respecting each other's family relationships."

Creating a Relationship Agreement (Without Feeling Like You're Signing Up for a Cell Phone Plan)

One of the most effective tools for navigating the transition is creating an explicit relationship agreement. Before you run screaming at the unromantic sound of that, know that this isn't about signing away your freedom or killing spontaneity. Think of it as a collaborative user manual for your unique relationship.

A good relationship agreement typically includes:

1. **Relationship Values and Vision**: The core principles guiding your relationship and what you're building together.

2. **Communication Agreements**: How you share information, express needs, and navigate disagreements.

3. **Boundary Frameworks**: How you maintain individual identities while building connections.

4. **Practical Functioning**: Day-to-day expectations around time together, communication frequency, and support.

5. **Growth Approach**: How you'll continue developing individually and as a couple.

6. **Amendment Process**: How you'll revise the agreement as your relationship evolves.

Elena described their process: "Creating our relationship agreement felt strange at first—like we were being too formal. But it led to the most honest and clarifying conversations we'd ever had. We discovered assumptions we'd made without realising it and created understandings that prevented many potential problems. It wasn't about restricting our relationship but ensuring we were building the same thing."

Maintaining Your Authentic Self (Because You've Worked Too Hard to Lose Yourself Now)

After all that self-connection work during your dating sabbatical, the last thing you want is to lose your authentic self as your relationship develops. Yet it happens so easily—often without noticing until you're waist-deep in self-compromise.

Several forces can pull you away from your authentic self:

- **The Approval Drive**: The natural desire for your partner's approval

- **The Merge Tendency**: That biochemical feeling of becoming one

- **The Conflict Avoidance Pull**: Fear of creating tension

- **Role Adaptation**: Unconsciously slipping into relationship roles

Jason recognised this pattern: "I'd been a chameleon in relationships—becoming whoever I thought my partner wanted. After my dating sabbatical, I was determined to maintain a connection with my authentic self even as I built a connection with my partner."

Try these authenticity protection practices:

- **Personal Check-In Ritual**: Regular practice of checking in with yourself

- **Authenticity Barometer**: Notice physical and emotional signals of self-disconnection

- **Differentiation Practice**: Distinguish between "relationship thinking" and "individual thinking"

- **Courageous Expression**: Express authentic thoughts even when uncomfortable

- **Separate Development**: Maintain investment in your individual growth

Thomas reflected: "Maintaining my authentic self while building deep connection was the breakthrough that made this relationship different from my previous ones. Instead of losing myself, I brought my whole self to it. Surprisingly, our connection became deeper and more satisfying than the false harmony I'd created through self-abandonment in the past."

Real Couples, Real Transitions

Let's look at how actual couples navigated this crucial stage:

Maya and Jordan: The Communication Approach They centred their transition on explicit communication:

- Weekly "relationship reflection" conversations

- Written documentation of agreements

- Regular check-ins about comfort with the pace

Their insight: "We discovered we had completely different definitions of relationship terms that could have created major confusion without our explicit conversations."

Carlos and Elena: The Graduated Commitment Approach They developed a framework with explicit steps:

- Phase 1: Exclusive Dating (Months 1-2)

- Phase 2: Preliminary Partnership (Months 3-5)

- Phase 3: Established Partnership (Months 6+)

Their insight: "Creating explicit relationship phases with clear agreements at each stage allowed us to develop commitment gradually rather than rushing or sliding."

Sophia and Tyler: The Values Foundation Approach Their transition centred on developing an explicit understanding of their relationship's core values:

- Creation of a relationship values statement

- Regular discussions about values in daily life
- Value-based decision-making

Their insight: "Knowing our relationship's foundational values gave us a framework for navigating all practical questions."

Alex and Mia: The Balanced Integration Approach They focused on balancing togetherness and independence:

- Creation of a "relationship pace comfort scale"
- Development of both "together rituals" and "separate space practices"
- Thoughtful integration of social circles

Their insight: "We discovered we had different natural preferences for togetherness versus independence. By discussing this directly, we created a balance that respected both needs."

The Science Behind Successful Transitions

Research shows relationships develop through distinct stages:

1. **Romance/Fusion Stage (Months 1-6)**: Intense feelings, idealisation, and merging
2. **Power Struggle/Differentiation (Months 6-24)**: Differences emerge, requiring navigation

3. **Stability/Recovery (Years 2-5)**: Established patterns and reduced conflict

4. **Commitment (Years 3-10)**: Conscious choice based on deep knowing

5. **Co-Creation/Synergy (Years 5+)**: Creating something beyond the relationship itself

How you handle the dating-to-relationship transition significantly impacts how you navigate these stages. Research shows couples who make explicit decisions rather than passively "sliding" through transitions show:

- Higher commitment to working through challenges

- Greater relationship confidence

- More effective communication

Dr Rachel Martinez sums it up: "The research consistently shows that intentional transition from dating to relationship significantly impacts long-term outcomes. Couples who navigate this period with explicit communication, balanced identity maintenance, and conscious commitment development establish foundations that support relationship health across multiple developmental stages."

Your Transition Toolkit: A Practical Exercise

Ready to put this into practice? Here's a structured exercise to create your own relationship agreement:

Preparation (Before Meeting)

- Individual reflection on values, needs, boundaries, expectations

- Schedule uninterrupted time together

- Choose a comfortable, neutral environment

- Come with an open, curious mindset

The Agreement Process (Together)

1. **Vision Sharing (30 min)**: Share your relationship visions and values

2. **Core Agreements (60 min)**: Discuss relationship definition, communication, boundaries, and functioning

3. **Specific Agreements (45 min)**: Create clear agreements in areas needing clarity

4. **Documentation (15 min)**: Record your agreements in whatever format works for you

5. **Implementation Planning (15 min)**: Discuss how you'll put these into practice

6. **Closing Appreciation (15 min)**: Express gratitude for the conversation and each other

Follow-Up Integration

- Two-week check-in on what's working and what needs adjustment

- One-month review for a more thorough assessment

- Ongoing evolution to ensure your agreement grows with your relationship

Carlos and Elena found this transformative: "Creating our relationship agreement felt awkward at first—like we were being too formal. But it led to the most honest, clarifying conversations we'd ever had. We discovered we'd been making completely different assumptions. These explicit conversations prevented many potential misunderstandings and created a foundation of clarity that supported our deepening connection."

As you navigate this transition, remember that this stage isn't just about changing your relationship status. It's about establishing the foundation that will support your relationship through all its future challenges and growth.

The attention, intentionality, and courage you bring to this transition will shape everything that follows. By approaching this crucial period with the care it deserves, you create not just a relationship label but the beginnings of a thriving partnership built on authentic connection, clear understanding, and mutual commitment to growth.

The relationship you build draws on all the self-development work you've done throughout your dating detox journey. Your reconnection with yourself, clear relationship vision, and strategic approach to dating have prepared you for this moment—creating a relationship that truly reflects your values and supports your vision of partnership.

And hey, if reading this chapter felt like work, remember that building something worthwhile always does. The good news? The foundation-building phase doesn't last forever, but the benefits of doing it well do.

Conclusion

When we began this journey together, you may have felt frustrated, confused, or hopeless about your dating life. Perhaps you were caught in cycles of attraction to unavailable partners, struggling to maintain healthy boundaries, or simply wondering why the same relationship patterns kept repeating despite your best intentions to find something different.

Wherever you started, you've now travelled through a comprehensive process of understanding, healing, and transforming your approach to dating and relationships. This wasn't just another collection of dating tips or tricks—it was a fundamental reimagining of how you relate to yourself, others, and the concept of love.

The Path You've Travelled

Let's take a moment to acknowledge the ground you've covered:

You broke your patterns in Part I by identifying the unconscious cycles shaping your relationship experiences. You explored the neuroscience of attraction, recognised your cognitive biases, and completed your dating detox period—creating the essential space for new patterns to emerge.

In Part II, you changed your life by developing a deeper relationship with yourself. You practised self-compassion, clarified your values, and designed a life that naturally attracts the kind of connection you truly want rather than what you've settled for in the past.

In Part III, you learned how to find your person through strategic approaches to dating, authentic connection skills, and thoughtful compatibility assessment. You developed the ability to navigate the crucial transition from dating to relationship in a way that establishes a solid foundation for lasting love.

This wasn't easy work. It required courage to look honestly at patterns you might have preferred to ignore. It demanded patience to sit with the discomfort of changing deeply ingrained habits. It took faith to believe that something different is possible when past experiences might have taught you otherwise.

From Reactive to Intentional

The fundamental shift you've made through this process is moving from reactive to intentional relationship patterns. Where you once might have been driven by unconscious attractions, unexamined beliefs, and automatic responses, you now have the awareness and tools to make conscious choices about your dating life.

This shift from reactive to intentional doesn't mean controlling outcomes or manipulating connections. It means bringing consciousness to a process that may have previously operated largely outside your awareness. It means recognising that while you can't control who you meet or how they respond, you absolutely can control how you approach dating, who you choose to invest in, and what boundaries you maintain.

The Dating Detox philosophy isn't about finding perfect partners or creating flawless relationships. It's about developing your capacity to create healthy connections based on authentic compatibility rather than familiar dysfunction. It's about engaging in dating and relationships from a place of wholeness rather than need, clarity rather than confusion, and intention rather than habit.

The Ongoing Practice

The work you've done isn't something you complete once and then move on from. It's more like learning a language or an instrument—a practice that continues to develop throughout your life. There will be moments of fluency alongside moments of returning to old patterns. There will be beautiful harmonies and occasional discordant notes.

This is normal. The goal isn't perfection but awareness and growth. It's not a failure when you notice yourself slipping back into familiar patterns—perhaps being drawn to someone who triggers old attachment wounds, compromising your boundaries to maintain a connection, or losing touch with your authentic self within a relationship. It's an opportunity to practice what you've learned with self-compassion rather than judgment.

The tools you've developed throughout this book—the self-connection practices, the pattern interruption techniques, the compatibility assessment frameworks—are resources you can return to repeatedly as your relationship journey unfolds. They're not one-time exercises but lifelong skills that grow stronger with continued practice.

Beyond the Book

As you move forward from these pages into your continued dating life, remember a few essential truths:

You are already whole. A romantic relationship can be a beautiful addition to your life, but it isn't what makes you complete or worthy. The work you've done to develop your relationship with yourself has established this foundation of wholeness that no external connection can provide.

Patterns can change. No matter how entrenched your relationship patterns have been, they can transform through conscious awareness and consistent practice. Your past does not determine your future unless you remain unconscious of its influence.

Progress isn't linear. There will be steps forward and steps back, moments of clarity and confusion. This doesn't mean the process isn't working—you're human, navigating one of the most complex aspects of human experience.

Community matters. Continue to cultivate the support system you developed during your dating sabbatical. Please share your insights, challenges, and growth with trusted others who can provide the most valuable perspective.

Love is both more straightforward and more complex than we make it. At its core, love is about seeing and being seen, accepting and accepting. The capacity for this connection lives within you already—it simply needs the right conditions to flourish.

Your Continuing Journey

As our time together ends, I want to acknowledge the courage it's taken to engage with this material so honestly. Examining your relationship patterns requires a willingness to look at aspects of yourself that might be uncomfortable or challenging.

Your staying with this process speaks volumes about your commitment to creating something different in your life.

Whether you're currently single, dating, or in the early stages of a relationship, the awareness and skills you've developed will serve you well. They'll help you recognise compatibility when you encounter it, maintain your boundaries when they're tested, and build connections based on genuine alignment rather than familiar chemistry alone.

Most importantly, they'll help you remember that you deserve a relationship that feels like coming home to yourself rather than losing yourself—one that supports your growth rather than requiring your diminishment, that sees your authenticity as a gift rather than an inconvenience.

The path to this kind of relationship isn't found primarily in the perfect dating strategy or in finding someone who checks all the right boxes. It's found in your continued commitment to knowing yourself, honouring your needs and values, and showing up authentically even when it feels vulnerable.

You've already begun this journey. The awareness you've developed can't be undone—even if you occasionally forget it, it remains within you, ready to be remembered. Trust this awareness. Trust yourself. And trust that the relationship patterns you've held for so long can truly transform into something healthier, more fulfilling, and more authentic than you might have believed possible.

Your capacity for genuine connection—with yourself and with others—is your birthright. May this book be just one step in your ongoing journey of claiming that birthright fully.

Thank you from the bottom of my heart for reading "The Dating Detox." By picking up this book, you've taken a brave first step toward breaking toxic dating cycles and finding the healthy love you deserve.

This journey of rewiring your heart isn't always easy, but it's worth it. I wrote this book because I believe everyone deserves to move out of their "type" and into their person, to find relationships that nourish rather than deplete.

Your commitment to your growth inspires me. Remember that transformation takes time, patience, and self-compassion. I'd love to hear your story as you implement these principles in your life. Your feedback and experiences help create a community of growth and support for others on similar paths.

If this book has made a difference, consider sharing your thoughts in an Amazon review. Your words might be exactly what someone else needs to hear to begin their dating detox journey.

Wishing you the love and connection you've always deserved,

Jed Lindsay

APPENDICES

Appendix A: The Complete Dating Detox Workbook

This comprehensive workbook consolidates the key exercises throughout the book, organised by section to support your ongoing practice.

PART I: Breaking Your Patterns

Relationship Pattern Mapping

- List your past 3-5 significant relationships/dating experiences

- For each, identify initial attraction triggers, the relationship dynamic, how it ended

- Circle commonalities across these experiences

- Identify your primary pattern type (Anxious Pursuer, Avoidant Distancer, Chaotic Roller-Coaster, etc.)

Chemistry Trigger Inventory

- When have you felt the strongest "chemistry" or attraction?

- What specific traits/behaviours triggered this response?

- How did this chemistry feeling manifest in your body?

- How do relationships with strong initial chemistry typically unfold?

Red Flag/Green Flag Personal Inventory

- List your red flags based on past experiences
- Identify green flags that indicate authentic compatibility
- Create your flag awareness checklist for future dating

Cognitive Bias Self-Assessment

- Identify which biases most affect your dating decisions:
    - Confirmation bias (seeing what you expect to see)
    - Halo effect (one positive quality overshadowing red flags)
    - Sunk cost fallacy (continuing based on past investment)
    - Optimism bias (assuming your situation is exceptional)
    - Familiarity bias (mistaking familiar for good)

Dating Sabbatical Planning

- Length of commitment (30, 60, or 90 days)
- Start and end dates: _____
- Specific behaviours you're detoxing from
- Support system during detox

- Daily practices during the detox period
- Weekly reflection questions

Pattern Interruption Protocol

- Identify your three most common unhealthy attraction triggers
- For each, create a specific interruption strategy
- Document your replacement behaviours plan

PART II: Changing Your Life

Self-Relationship Assessment

- Rate (1-10) how you treat yourself in:
    - Self-talk tone and content
    - Honouring your own boundaries
    - Keeping commitments to yourself
    - Meeting your emotional needs
    - Appreciating your strengths and progress

Core Values Clarification

- Identify your top 5-7 relationship values
- For each, define what it looks like in practice
- Rank in order of priority for relationship decisions

Self-Dating Calendar

- Daily mini dates (5-15 minutes): schedule specific times

- Weekly connection dates (1-2 hours): schedule specific activities

- Monthly deep-dive dates: schedule and plan content

Relationship Vision Creation

- Describe the quality of the relationship you want to create

- What would daily life in this relationship include?

- How would challenges be navigated?

- What growth would this relationship support?

Support Network Development

- List your current support resources

- Identify gaps in your support system

- Create a plan to build needed support

- Develop your accountability structure

PART III: Finding Your Person

Strategic Dating Plan

- Channel strategy (which dating method is for you)

- Quality approach implementation
- Simultaneous connection limits
- Dating boundary framework
- Regular assessment schedule

Connection Skills Practice Plan

- Weekly vulnerability practice
- Curious questioning development
- Presence listening exercises
- Connection pattern recognition

Compatibility Assessment Framework

- Values compatibility checklist
- Emotional compatibility indicators
- Practical compatibility assessment
- Physical compatibility reflection
- Red flag vs. growth opportunity guidance

Relationship Agreement Template

- Communication agreements
- Boundary framework

- Practical expectations
- Growth and development approach
- Amendment process

Appendix B: Resources for Further Healing

Books for Deepening Your Understanding

Attachment and Relationship Patterns:

- *Attached: The New Science of Adult Attachment and How It Can Help You Find—and Keep—Love* by Amir Levine and Rachel Heller

- *Wired for Love: How Understanding Your Partner's Brain and Attachment Style Can Help You Defuse Conflict and Build a Secure Relationship* by Stan Tatkin

- *Insecure in Love: How Anxious Attachment Can Make You Feel Jealous, Needy, and Worried and What You Can Do About It* by Leslie Becker-Phelps

Self-Relationship Development:

- *Self-Compassion: The Proven Power of Being Kind to Yourself* by Kristin Neff

- *Set Boundaries, Find Peace: A Guide to Reclaiming Yourself* by Nedra Glover Tawwab

- *The Path to Authenticity: Discovering Your True Self and Building Meaningful Relationships* by Stephen Cope

Dating and Relationship Skills:

- *Eight Dates: Essential Conversations for a Lifetime of Love* by John Gottman and Julie Schwartz Gottman

- *How to Not Die Alone: The Surprising Science That Will Help You Find Love* by Logan Ury

- *The State of Affairs: Rethinking Infidelity* by Esther Perel

Healing Past Relationship Wounds:

- *The Journey from Abandonment to Healing* by Susan Anderson

- *Getting Past Your Breakup: How to Turn a Devastating Loss into the Best Thing That Ever Happened to You* by Susan J. Elliott

- *Emotional First Aid: Healing Rejection, Guilt, Failure, and Other Everyday Hurts* by Guy Winch

Podcasts for Ongoing Learning

- **Where Should We Begin?** by Esther Perel Hear real couples navigate relationship challenges with master therapist Esther Perel

- **Dear Relationships** by Dr. Alexandra Solomon Research-based insights on relationships from a clinical psychologist and relationship educator

- **The Baggage Reclaim Sessions** by Natalie Lue Practical guidance for breaking unhealthy patterns and building self-esteem in relationships

- **Deeper Dating** by Ken Page Explores an approach to dating that values authenticity and self-compassion over game-playing

- **Unlocking Us** by Brené Brown Thought-provoking conversations on vulnerability, courage, and human connection

Online Resources and Communities

- **The Gottman Institute** Research-based resources for relationship health and development **www.gottman.com**

- **The Attachment Project** Assessment tools and educational resources for understanding attachment patterns **www.attachmentproject.com**

- **Authentic Connection Community** Online community for support in developing healthy relationship patterns **www.authenticconnection.org**

- **Mind Body Green: Relationships** Articles and courses on mindful approaches to dating and relationships **www.mindbodygreen.com/relationships**

- **Modern Love Column and Podcast** Thoughtful explorations of contemporary relationship experiences **www.nytimes.com/column/modern-love**

Appendix C: Research References and Studies Cited

This appendix provides academic citations for the key research referenced throughout the book, organized by topic for those interested in exploring the science more deeply.

Attachment Theory and Adult Relationships

- Hazan, C., & Shaver, P. (1987). Romantic love conceptualized as an attachment process. *Journal of Personality and Social Psychology, 52*(3), 511-524.

- Mikulincer, M., & Shaver, P. R. (2007). *Attachment in adulthood: Structure, dynamics, and change.* Guilford Press.

- Levine, A., & Heller, R. S. F. (2010). *Attached: The new science of adult attachment and how it can help you find—and keep—love.* Penguin.

- Johnson, S. M. (2008). *Hold me tight: Seven conversations for a lifetime of love.* Little, Brown Spark.

Neuroscience of Attraction and Relationship Formation

- Fisher, H. E., Aron, A., & Brown, L. L. (2006). Romantic love: A mammalian brain system for mate choice. *Philosophical Transactions of the Royal Society B: Biological Sciences, 361*(1476), 2173-2186.

- Acevedo, B. P., Aron, A., Fisher, H. E., & Brown, L. L. (2012). Neural correlates of long-term intense romantic love. *Social Cognitive and Affective Neuroscience, 7*(2), 145-159.

- Young, L. J., & Wang, Z. (2004). The neurobiology of pair bonding. *Nature Neuroscience, 7*(10), 1048-1054.

- Ortigue, S., Bianchi-Demicheli, F., Hamilton, A. F. D. C., & Grafton, S. T. (2007). The neural basis of love as a subliminal prime: An event-related functional magnetic resonance imaging study. *Journal of Cognitive Neuroscience, 19*(7), 1218-1230.

Relationship Development and Success Predictors

- Gottman, J. M., & Silver, N. (2015). *The seven principles for making marriage work.* Harmony.

- Knee, C. R., Patrick, H., & Lonsbary, C. (2003). Implicit theories of relationships: Orientations toward evaluation and cultivation. *Personality and Social Psychology Review, 7*(1), 41-55.

- Stanley, S. M., Rhoades, G. K., & Markman, H. J. (2006). Sliding versus deciding: Inertia and the premarital cohabitation effect. *Family Relations, 55*(4), 499-509.

- Fincham, F. D., & Beach, S. R. (2010). Marriage in the new millennium: A decade in review. *Journal of Marriage and Family, 72*(3), 630-649.

Communication and Connection Research

- Gottman, J. M. (1994). *What predicts divorce? The relationship between marital processes and marital outcomes.* Lawrence Erlbaum Associates.

- Driver, J. L., & Gottman, J. M. (2004). Daily marital interactions and positive affect during marital conflict among newlywed couples. *Family Process, 43*(3), 301-314.

- Laurenceau, J. P., Barrett, L. F., & Pietromonaco, P. R. (1998). Intimacy as an interpersonal process: The importance of self-disclosure, partner disclosure, and perceived partner responsiveness in interpersonal exchanges. *Journal of Personality and Social Psychology, 74*(5), 1238-1251.

- Gable, S. L., Gonzaga, G. C., & Strachman, A. (2006). Will you be there for me when things go right? Supportive responses to positive event disclosures. *Journal of Personality and Social Psychology, 91*(5), 904-917.

Self-Relationship and Well-Being

- Neff, K. D., & Beretvas, S. N. (2013). The role of self-compassion in romantic relationships. *Self and Identity, 12*(1), 78-98.

- Deci, E. L., & Ryan, R. M. (2008). Self-determination theory: A macrotheory of human motivation, development, and health. *Canadian Psychology/Psychologie Canadienne, 49*(3), 182-185.

- La Guardia, J. G., Ryan, R. M., Couchman, C. E., & Deci, E. L. (2000). Within-person variation in security of attachment: A self-determination theory perspective on attachment, need fulfillment, and well-being. *Journal of Personality and Social Psychology, 79*(3), 367-384.

- Baker, L. R., & McNulty, J. K. (2011). Self-compassion and relationship maintenance: The moderating roles of conscientiousness and gender. *Journal of Personality and Social Psychology, 100*(5), 853-873.

Habit Formation and Change

- Wood, W., & Neal, D. T. (2007). A new look at habits and the habit-goal interface. *Psychological Review, 114*(4), 843-863.

- Lally, P., Van Jaarsveld, C. H., Potts, H. W., & Wardle, J. (2010). How are habits formed: Modelling habit formation in the real world. *European Journal of Social Psychology, 40*(6), 998-1009.

- Duhigg, C. (2012). *The power of habit: Why we do what we do in life and business*. Random House.

- Clear, J. (2018). *Atomic habits: An easy & proven way to build good habits & break bad ones*. Penguin.

Decision-Making and Cognitive Biases

- Kahneman, D. (2011). *Thinking, fast and slow*. Farrar, Straus and Giroux.

- Ariely, D. (2008). *Predictably irrational: The hidden forces that shape our decisions*. HarperCollins.

- Tversky, A., & Kahneman, D. (1974). Judgment under uncertainty: Heuristics and biases. *Science, 185*(4157), 1124-1131.

- Samuelson, W., & Zeckhauser, R. (1988). Status quo bias in decision making. *Journal of Risk and Uncertainty, 1*(1), 7-59.

Online Dating Research

- Finkel, E. J., Eastwick, P. W., Karney, B. R., Reis, H. T., & Sprecher, S. (2012). Online dating: A critical analysis from the perspective of psychological science. *Psychological Science in the Public Interest, 13*(1), 3-66.

- Rosenfeld, M. J., Thomas, R. J., & Hausen, S. (2019). Disintermediating your friends: How online dating in the United States displaces other ways of meeting. *Proceedings of the National Academy of Sciences, 116*(36), 17753-17758.

- Eastwick, P. W., & Hunt, L. L. (2014). Relational mate value: Consensus and uniqueness in romantic evaluations. *Journal of Personality and Social Psychology, 106*(5), 728-751.

- Hitsch, G. J., Hortaçsu, A., & Ariely, D. (2010). Matching and sorting in online dating. *American Economic Review, 100*(1), 130-163.

Appendix D: Dating Detox Community Resources

Finding support for your Dating Detox journey can significantly enhance your success. Here are resources for connecting with others on similar paths.

Online Communities

Dating Detox Forum: An online community specifically for readers of this book to share experiences, ask questions, and support each other's journeys. www.datingdetoxbook.com/community

Authentic Dating Alliance A moderated online community focused on developing healthy relationship patterns and authentic connections. www.authenticdatingalliance.org

Pattern Breakers Network Support community for those working to break unhealthy relationship cycles. www.patternbreakers.net

Secure Attachment Development Group This online community is focused specifically on developing earned secure attachment. www.secureattachmentgroup.org

In-Person Support Options

Relationship Pattern Transformation Groups Therapist-led groups available in many cities, focusing on changing unhealthy relationship patterns. Search: "relationship pattern group [your city]"

Adult Children of Dysfunctional Families Groups Support groups for those working to break intergenerational patterns. www.adultchildren.org

Codependency Recovery Groups For those working on boundary development and self-relationship. www.coda.org

Mindful Dating Meetups Local groups practicing intentional approaches to dating and relationship development. Search Meetup.com: "mindful dating [your city]"

Professional Support Resources

Therapist Directories Find therapists specializing in relationship patterns:

- Psychology Today Therapist Directory
- GoodTherapy.org
- TherapyDen.com

Relationship Coaches For those seeking coaching rather than therapy:

- Relationship Coaching Network
- International Coaching Federation Directory (search for relationship specialists)

Dating Detox Certified Practitioners Professionals specifically trained in the Dating Detox methodology: **www.datingdetoxcertified.com**

Virtual Workshops and Courses

The Complete Dating Detox Course An expanded online course based on the book, with video instruction and guided exercises. **www.datingdetoxcourse.com**

Attachment Rewiring Workshop 8-week online program focused specifically on developing secure attachment patterns. **www.attachmentrewiring.com**

The Boundaries Breakthrough 6-week course on developing and maintaining healthy relationship boundaries. **www.boundariesbreakthrough.com**

Authentic Connection Masterclass Intensive workshop on developing deeper connection skills in dating and relationships. www.authenticconnectionmasterclass.com

Appendix E: Troubleshooting Common Dating Challenges

This section addresses specific challenges you might encounter in implementing your Dating Detox and provides targeted solutions.

Challenge: Dealing with Dating App Burnout

Signs of burnout:

- Feeling dread when opening dating apps
- Cynical or dismissive attitude toward potential matches
- Decreased effort in conversations
- Feeling exhausted rather than excited about dates

Solutions:

1. **Implement strict usage boundaries:**
    - Limit app usage to specific times (e.g., 30 minutes, 3x weekly)
    - Turn off notifications to prevent constant triggering
    - Delete apps from your phone on designated "app-free" days

2. **Quality over quantity approach:**
    - Limit active conversations to 2-3 at a time
    - Be more selective with initial matching
    - Invest more deeply in promising connections

3. **Channel diversification:**
    - Alternate between app dating and other meeting methods
    - Take 2-week breaks from apps when burnout intensifies
    - Use different apps that require more thoughtful engagement

4. **Mindset reset:**
    - Implement a pre-swiping centering practice
    - Maintain realistic expectations about response rates
    - Remember that app dating is just one tool, not the entire process

Challenge: Maintaining Boundaries with Potential Partners

Common boundary challenges:

- Difficulty saying no to date requests when not interested
- Feeling pressured to move faster than comfortable
- Compromising values to maintain someone's interest
- Overaccommodating others' preferences at your expense

Solutions:

1. **Script preparation:**
    - Develop and practice specific boundary scripts in advance
    - Example: "I've enjoyed getting to know you, but I don't feel the connection I'm looking for"
    - Example: "I'd like to take physical intimacy more slowly so we can build emotional connection first"

2. **Boundary reinforcement system:**
    - Share your boundaries with an accountability partner

- Check in after dates to review boundary maintenance
- Celebrate successful boundary holding (even when uncomfortable)

3. **Red flag response protocol:**
    - Identify your personal boundary non-negotiables
    - Create specific response plans for common pressure tactics
    - Practice disengaging when boundaries aren't respected

4. **Value reconnection practice:**
    - Before dates, review your core values and boundaries
    - After feeling boundary pressure, reconnect with your "why"
    - Remember that maintained boundaries attract compatible partners

Challenge: Distinguishing Between Fear and Intuition

The confusion:

- Not knowing if hesitation comes from unhealthy patterns or genuine intuition

- Difficulty separating attachment triggers from compatibility concerns

- Confusion between reasonable caution and fear-based avoidance

Solutions:

1. **The body-mind differentiation:**

    - Fear often manifests as constriction, tightness, or anxiety in the body

    - Intuition typically presents as a calm knowing or clarity

    - Practice the body scan technique to distinguish these sensations

2. **The third-person perspective:**

    - Describe the situation as if explaining it to a friend

    - Ask yourself: "What would I advise someone else in this situation?"

    - Notice if your perspective shifts when removing personal emotion

3. **The pattern-checking process:**

    - Ask: "Does this concern fit my established pattern or is it unique to this situation?"

- Look for concrete behaviors rather than interpretations

- Consider whether the concern relates to core values versus preferences

4. **The time-testing approach:**

    - Give non-emergency concerns time before acting

    - Notice if the feeling intensifies or clarifies with time

    - Journal about the concern for 3 days before making decisions

Challenge: Navigating Chemistry vs. Compatibility Confusion

The confusion:

- Strong attraction to incompatible people
- Dismissing compatible partners due to "lack of spark"
- Difficulty distinguishing between anxiety and authentic attraction

Solutions:

1. **The chemistry deconstruction exercise:**

    - When feeling strong chemistry, identify specific physical sensations

- Note whether these sensations resemble anxiety responses
- Compare to how you feel with people who provide consistent security

2. **The delayed judgment approach:**

    - Commit to 3 dates before assessing chemistry with compatible matches
    - Look for growing comfort and connection rather than immediate intensity
    - Notice whether interest increases or decreases across multiple meetings

3. **The attraction development practice:**

    - Deliberately focus on attractive qualities in compatible partners
    - Create date experiences that foster connection rather than performance
    - Practice physical presence and full attention to allow attraction to develop

4. **The chemistry contextualization:**

    - Remind yourself of previous high-chemistry relationships that failed
    - Review research on chemistry versus long-term satisfaction

- Distinguish between chemistry and compatibility in specific terms

Challenge: Managing Dating Rejection

Common challenges:

- Taking rejection as evidence of unworthiness
- Allowing rejection to reinforce negative self-beliefs
- Becoming risk-averse after rejection experiences
- Overanalyzing reasons for rejection

Solutions:

1. **The rejection reframe practice:**
   - View rejection as compatibility information, not personal failure
   - Remember that rejection often reflects the other person's issues and limitations
   - Consider whether you would actually want someone who doesn't want you

2. **The self-compassion protocol:**
   - Acknowledge the pain of rejection without judgment
   - Remind yourself that rejection is a universal human experience

- Treat yourself with the same kindness you would offer a friend

3. **The resilience-building system:**
    - Develop a post-rejection self-care ritual
    - Connect with supportive people after rejection experiences
    - Review evidence of your worth independent of dating outcomes

4. **The growth extraction:**
    - After the emotional impact has reduced, assess what can be learned
    - Distinguish between useful feedback and subjective preference
    - Integrate valid insights without internalizing others' limitations

Challenge: Sustaining Motivation During Dating Plateaus

Common challenges:

- Frustration with lack of promising connections
- Temptation to return to unhealthy patterns for quick validation
- Doubt about whether healthier approaches actually work

- Dating fatigue without apparent progress

Solutions:

1. **The success recalibration:**
    - Redefine success beyond finding a partner
    - Celebrate growth in boundary-setting, authentic expression, etc.
    - Acknowledge progress in avoiding unhealthy patterns

2. **The inspiration renewal:**
    - Connect with others who have successfully transformed patterns
    - Review your relationship vision to reconnect with your "why"
    - Take breaks to restore energy without abandoning the process

3. **The process trust development:**
    - Review evidence that healthier approaches lead to better outcomes
    - Remember that quality connections are rarer but more valuable
    - Recognize that time spent single is better than time in unhealthy relationships

4. **The plateau productivity plan:**

    o Use plateau periods to deepen self-development work

    o Engage in activities that build relationship skills indirectly

    o Focus on creating a fulfilling life that a relationship would complement

Final Note on Troubleshooting

Remember that challenges in implementing your Dating Detox don't indicate failure—they're normal parts of the transformation process. Each challenge successfully navigated strengthens your new patterns and builds confidence in your ability to create healthier relationship experiences.

The most successful Dating Detox journeys aren't those without difficulties but those where difficulties become opportunities for deeper learning and complete pattern transformation. Be patient with yourself, maintain a connection with your support resources, and trust that each challenge navigated brings you closer to the authentic, fulfilling relationship you deserve.

Published by Eden Ray Publishing LTD

www.ingramcontent.com/pod-product-compliance
Lightning Source LLC
Chambersburg PA
CBHW020339010526
44119CB00048B/530